Visual E
Reflection Handbook

Syed Fahad Gilani
Mike Gillespie
James Hart
Benny K. Mathew
Andy Olsen

Wrox Press Ltd. ®

Visual Basic .NET Reflection Handbook

© 2002 Wrox Press

First published September 2002

Published by Wrox Press Ltd,
Arden House, 1102 Warwick Road, Acocks Green,
Birmingham, B27 6BH
United Kingdom
Printed in the United States
ISBN 1-86100-759-0

Trademark Acknowledgements

Wrox has endeavored to provide trademark information about all the companies and products mentioned in this book by the appropriate use of capitals. However, Wrox cannot guarantee the accuracy of this information.

Credits

Authors
Syed Fahad Gilani
Mike Gillespie
James Hart
Benny K. Mathew
Andy Olsen

Technical Reviewers
Michael Corning
Damien Foggon
Mark Horner
Phil Powers-DeGeorge
Scott Robertson
David Schultz
Erick Sgarbi

Proofreader
Susan Nettleton

Managing Editor
Jan Kolasinski

Commissioning Editor
James Hart

Technical Editor
Christian Peak

Project Manager
Beckie Stones

Index
Michael Brinkman
Andrew Criddle

Production and Layout
Sarah Hall

Cover
Natalie O'Donnell

About the Authors

Syed Fahad Gilani

A 22 year old with a Bachelor's Degree, Fahad's doing a Masters Program in Computer Engineering at the Australian National University. Living in Pakistan all his life, he's been into the programming scenario for the last thirteen years, managing to sell his first program at the age of ten. Over the years, he has worked in a number of software development companies and on numerous private projects in various roles, which have been a great source of income. His expertise includes anything that's possible and anything that would manage to keep him awake through the night. Currently Fahad is running a small software development company, teaching, training and writing. If not working, you'd find him playing his guitar, jogging, eating or back-flipping. Fahad wishes to keep a horse one day.

Many thanks go to Wrox for all the support and encouragement they've given me. I'd like to thank Christian Peak especially, for bearing with me, and making things come easier.

Once again, it's been a great pleasure writing for this book. I'd like to apologize to my mother for making her miss out on me, and to the rest of my family for being there always. Thank you Dev, for all your support, I needed it.

Mike Gillespie

Mike Gillespie is currently the Director of Software Development for the CoolTel Telemetry group at Chart Industries. CoolTel is a provider of web based telemetry and routing solutions for monitoring and routing the delivery of liquid carbon dioxide to restaurants and oxygen for medical therapy. While at CoolTel, Mike co-designed a flexible web architecture written in VB6 and ASP to allow CoolTel to quickly customize its site for each market segment.

Outside of work, Mike enjoys many activities, such as astrophotography, boat building, and home brewing. Mike graduated from the University of Notre Dame with a degree in Computer Science.

I'd like to thank the staff at Wrox, especially Christian Peak and Beckie Stones and the technical reviewers. I'd also like to thank Pete Stromquist for working with me at Chart and referring me to Wrox. Thanks also go out to David Kalthoff for his help with .NET.

James Hart

James is an author, programmer, and technical communicator at Wrox in Birmingham, UK. As a member of the editorial team he has been helping others to teach programming concepts for the last three years, and writing books for the last eighteen months. Originally a Java developer (well, originally a ZX Basic developer, but that hardly counts), he is now applying his experiences with Sun's object-oriented platform to the .NET Framework. His current square-peg in a round-hole project involves trying to teach his Mac to program ASP.NET applications.

When not getting to grips with a new programming paradigm, James devotes his time to Italian food, radio controlled gadgets, and trying not to forget how to play guitar.

Thanks to my Dad, for not disowning me even though I now program with Microsoft technologies; to my Mum, for the cake; to my in-laws, for Chris; and to Chris, for the rest.

Benny K. Mathew

Benny is a programmer for Thomson Financial Research in Bangalore, India. He enjoys working for this company and attributes it to his manager Rameshwar Prasad, who constantly motivates him to think innovatively, and to his director Gourav Srivastava who is doing everything he can to make it a great place to work.

Benny has been programming with a passion since High School. He completed his Master's in Computer Applications. He has experience in OOP, Java, VB6, SQL Server, ASP and is fascinated by the .NET Technology. You can reach him by e-mail at benny_k_mathew@yahoo.com.

> *I'd like to dedicate this work to my parents, for making me what I am today, for their unconditional love, care and sacrifice, and for their confidence in me. To my wife Seno, for giving me support and encouragement in all my endeavours.*

> *I'd like to thank the people at Wrox, especially, Adam Ryland, Beckie Stones, Christian Peak, and James Hart for their cooperation and confidence in me.*

Andy Olsen

Andy is a freelance consultant engaged in training, consultancy, and development work in Microsoft .NET and related technologies. Andy studied Physics at Southampton University in England, and began his professional life as a C developer. As the 1990s came and went, Andy migrated into C++, Visual Basic, Java, and OO Analysis and Design using UML. Andy has been using Microsoft development tools and technologies since 1987, and has fond memories and many tall stories to tell of times gone by.

Andy now lives by the sea in Swansea, with his wife Jayne, and their children Emily and Thomas. Andy is a keen football and rugby supporter, and enjoys running and skiing (badly). You can reach Andy at andyo@olsensoft.com.

VB.NET

Reflection

Handbook

Table of Contents

Table of Contents

VB.NET

Reflection

Handbook

Introduction

Introduction

One of the great things about .NET is its refined use of metadata to describe the contents of assemblies. Let's make it clear: the use of metadata to describe components is not an idea new to .NET (COM used it too). However, many of the problems associated with the use of metadata in COM/COM+, such as metadata getting out of sync with a component, have been ironed out in .NET.

.NET also takes the use of metadata a step further. It allows you to search through and examine assembly metadata programmatically at runtime – a process known as **reflection**. And that's not all: after your code has used reflection and metadata to find the classes it's interested in, it can create instances of them, invoke their methods, and manipulate their members.

Impressed? You should be, because this ability to change the classes and methods used by your programs dynamically at runtime is a powerful tool. It can make your programs far more flexible and extensible. And customizable too! Say you wanted to create an application that would allow users to plug custom components into it. As you write and compile your application, you may have absolutely no idea which classes these components will use – how can you code for that? Reflection is the key, because it allows your application to examine the plug-in at runtime and find the answers for itself.

Now, we've assumed that, being a VB.NET programmer, you're pretty interested in creating flexible, extensible, customizable programs, and therefore you're now curious to know more about reflection. And this, of course, is where this VB.NET Reflection Handbook comes in.

Who is this Book for?

All of the books in the VB.NET Handbook Series are targeted at practicing Visual Basic .NET developers, who need to learn more to complete a specific task. The books assume that you have already written, compiled, and run VB.NET code, and that you are familiar with your chosen development tool. In this book, we consider when and how we can use the .NET Reflection API to make our applications more flexible and customizable.

Book Outline

Written with Visual Basic .NET developers in mind, this book explores reflection in depth, introducing program scenarios where it is the best or only option, and explaining how to use the classes of the Reflection API effectively and safely.

Chapter by chapter, here's what to expect:

❑ *Chapter 1 – Flexible Programming*

We start off our tour of reflection by discussing how the kind of object binding used by your code can affect its flexibility. In particular, we discuss the advantages and disadvantages of dynamic (runtime) binding, and we highlight the Reflection API as the mechanism to implement this.

❑ *Chapter 2 – Examining Assemblies, Objects, and Types*

Having introduced the Reflection API on a conceptual level, we now start to use the classes of the API to perform reflection in our VB.NET programs. In this chapter we show you how to examine the metadata of an assembly, so that our programs can dynamically locate the classes they need at runtime.

❑ *Chapter 3 – Using Objects*

The next step is to make use of the classes we find using reflection, and so in this chapter we go beyond the passive use of reflection in the previous chapter, and find out how to dynamically invoke methods and modify class data reflectively.

❑ *Chapter 4 – Creating Objects*

In this chapter we move to the next level, learning how to load assemblies dynamically and how to instantiate objects using reflection. We also discuss the advantages of using the Abstract Factory design pattern in our applications, and then show how we can combine this with reflection in order to create applications that will dynamically load core modules.

❑ *Chapter 5 – Attributes*

Attributes allow us to add and control the metadata associated with our classes. In this chapter we dive into the world of attribute-based programming, explaining how to use existing attributes and code new ones, and discussing when we should want to use them.

❑ *Chapter 6 – The .NET Component Model*

In the last chapter we tie together all the strands from the previous chapters. We show you how you can create highly flexible, customizable, and extensible generic applications, through the effective use of reflection, attributes, and classes from the System.ComponentModel namespace.

We have also included an appendix that contains support and code download details for this book. For more information about Wrox in general, visit our homepage at http://www.wrox.com/

VB.NET

Reflection

Handbook

1

Flexible Programming

This is a book, as the title says, about the .NET Reflection API. But rather than concentrating on describing what reflection is, we'll be spending most of our time looking at what it's actually for. So, this book is as much about dynamic programming as it is about reflection.

By dynamic programming, what we mean is developing applications that are flexible, dynamic, and extensible; programs whose behavior can be modified after they were written, after they've been installed, even while they are running.

We'll see how we can make applications less tightly coupled, and more modular. We'll look at how we can build flexible base classes that bestow powerful functionality on classes derived from them. We'll see how to use attributes to make information about our programs available to other pieces of code. And we'll examine .NET's component model, a system for enabling diverse objects to be treated as interchangeable blocks, which is the basis of all .NET user interface technologies.

In this first chapter, we'll take a look at some theoretical issues that place the Reflection API into context. We'll define reflection, look into some other key terms that we'll encounter in the book, and see why reflection is needed.

Reflection Defined

Reflection is easily described in terms of what it enables us to do, and indeed how it does it. What's harder is explaining why you might want to do it. But before we attempt the latter, let's take a shot at the first two. First, what is reflection for?

> **Reflection is a mechanism for examining, manipulating, and creating objects dynamically, at runtime.**

Reflection lets us examine an object, determine its type, discover information about that type, find out what members the type has, and manipulate or modify those members. It also allows us to examine assemblies, find what types they define, and create new instances of those types.

Isn't that exactly what we do anyway when we're programming? Well, yes – except that when we write code that calls a method, creates an object, or modifies a property, we're only able to take into account information that we know about at the time we're writing the code. Reflection allows us to take into account information that isn't available at compile-time, which is only available at runtime. We can only compile method calls to methods that have already been written. We can only refer to types that exist at the time we're coding. Reflection allows us to access any method of any type, even if it hasn't been written yet.

So, second, how does it work?

> **Reflection accesses metadata stored in .NET assemblies to discover information about the original code.**

This means that in order to provide the information about an object's type, its methods, properties and so on, reflection relies on information about the object's code which was encoded into the assembly by the .NET compiler. This metadata (data about data) can also be used to discover a great deal about the assembly, the types it defines, and the resources it requires.

So, with the easy questions out of the way, on to the big one: What can we use it for?

What is Reflection For?

Many objects we use in our programs represent real world entities external to our program – a window, a button, a purchase order. Others represent constructs we create within our program to help order these real-world entities – a hashtable, a database connection pool, a focus manager. Reflection is an interesting API because its objects represent the actual entities that make up our application itself – a type, a method, an assembly.

Reflection is .NET's way of letting our code look at itself, and examine and manipulate objects not as windows, or purchase orders, or hashtables, but as instances of a .NET type, defined in a .NET assembly. Since *every* object we encounter in our code is an instance of a .NET type, this means we can write code that can process *any* object.

To give an example, it's interesting to note that there are over 140 types in the .NET class library that define a property called Name. In almost all cases, this returns a String, representing the name of the entity it represents. You've probably coded a few classes with a property like this yourself, in fact. In the course of profiling or debugging an application, it might become necessary to track exactly which objects are being created, and we might code a method to output a diagnostic message. It might be nice to include the name of the object, where one is provided, to ease debugging. In VB.NET, by default we are allowed to write code like this:

```
Public Sub ShowDiagnostic(o As Object)
    Console.WriteLine(o.Name)
End Sub
```

This takes advantage of VB.NET's late binding facility (and should be familiar coding style to VB6 programmers). We'll look at exactly what we mean by late binding in a moment. For now, consider it as meaning that we can call any property or method on an instance of type Object, because .NET will work out whether the underlying object has the method or property and access it if it can. Of course, if there is no such method or property, the binding will fail, and an error will occur.

However, if we turn Option Strict on, the code won't compile. This is because System.Object doesn't define a Name property, and there's no guarantee that there will be a property of that name on the object o. Accessing this property on an object that doesn't have a Name would cause an error, and since we have no error trapping in place, it'll break our program. To prevent this very likely runtime error, VB.NET catches the error at compile time.

Option Strict disables VB.NET's syntactic late binding facility. It's recommended best practice that you turn Option Strict on in all your code, because for every occasion like this one, where the call to an undefined property is deliberate, there are a hundred situations where you could just mistype the name of the called method, and Option Strict lets the compiler help you catch them. This line would compile with Option Strict off:

```
Public Sub ShowDiagnostic(o As Object)
    Console.WriteLine(o.ToStrin())
End Sub
```

Reflection, however, lets us explicitly write code that says, "does this object's type define a `Name` property that returns a `String`? If so, display it, if not, don't". This will work whether `Option Strict` is turned on or off. It makes the questions that we're asking explicit, and suggests that an object not having a `Name` property is a normal, expected possibility, not an error condition. So, reflection provides a clean, logical way to write code that performs late binding, even under `Option Strict`.

Late binding of this sort allows us to develop coding **protocols**. A protocol is a set of rules that define the behavior of a set of types. A type that obeys all the rules is said to follow the protocol. For example, having a property called `Name` that returns a `String` is a protocol – one which 140 or so .NET classes follow. .NET provides a means for codifying a protocol of this sort into an interface, but it doesn't always allow the required flexibility. For example, imagine .NET has an interface `INamed` like this:

```
Public Interface INamed
   Public Property Name As String
End Interface
```

If all the classes that define a `Name` property implemented this interface, would that allow us to write typesafe code to manipulate all of .NET's named objects? Well, yes, but at the expense of forcing all of the classes that implement the interface to make their `Name` property readable *and writable*. Many of the .NET name properties are, not surprisingly, read-only. So we couldn't use an interface to impose a uniform type convention on those names. In this situation, we are left relying on defining a protocol, which we can only make use of through late binding.

.NET itself uses protocols. If a type has a `Shared Main()` method with one of a fixed set of signatures, it can be used as an entry point. Any type that defines a method called `GetEnumerator()` that returns an object of a type that has a method called `MoveNext()` that returns a `Boolean`, and a method called `Current()` that returns an object of the original type, is regarded by .NET as following the collection protocol. Instances of such classes can be iterated by a `For Each` statement. You can determine whether an object follows the entry point or collection protocol yourself using reflection, and you can call the methods using late binding – preferably through reflection.

These protocols are interesting, because again, they can't be defined by an interface. The first defines a shared method that a type must have. Interfaces can't define shared methods. The second defines a method signature in terms of the characteristics of the type it should return, which depend on the initial type. An interface can only define a method signature with a fixed return type. Reflection provides the only way of binding to such methods.

Reflection also allows us to bind to methods in other ways that VB.NET's syntactic late binding doesn't allow, as we'll see a little later on.

8

Reflection's late binding, unlike VB.NET's syntactic late binding, is not only used to select a method or property – it can be used to select an assembly or type as well.

Here's a simple example we've all encountered. An application is built to be modular, with extension modules sold separately, possibly by completely independent vendors. It might be a drawing package, with visual effects provided by extension modules; it might be an IDE, with different language compilers supplied separately; or it could be a mail server, with filter or protocol modules available as configurable plug-ins. Whatever the program's particular requirements, the problem is one of getting a core application to recognize and interoperate with code that it was not compiled against, containing classes whose names it doesn't know, and seamlessly integrate it.

Reflection provides the mechanism for doing this, and we'll look at how we can make such systems in Chapter 4, *Creating Objects*. The basis for the solution is to have all the modules provide a class that implements a particular interface, then to use reflection to load the assembly containing the module, and seek out that class. Having found it, we can use reflection to create an instance, and then use it just like any object that implements the interface.

Other examples of reflection in action are provided by .NET itself. The dynamic web technology ASP.NET, for example, is just a .NET program running alongside your web server. When the server receives a request for a web page ending in .aspx, it passes the request on to the ASP.NET program. ASP.NET identifies the file or files containing the code that makes up a page, and if it hasn't done so before, compiles them into a .NET assembly, containing one or more .NET classes, containing the code that makes up the logic required to deliver the requested page. The mechanism that ASP.NET then uses to create an instance of the correct class to service a particular request relies in part on reflection. The ASP.NET page classes inherit from a .NET base class called Page that contains functionality that uses reflection to create all the controls that make up the page, hook up event handlers, and set up the necessary initial properties on all of the items that make up the page. Every ASP.NET page you write is a new class, but the ASP.NET runtime uses reflection to ensure that you don't have to duplicate a lot of tedious boilerplate code in every page. In this case, reflection provides mechanisms for code reuse far beyond the basic system of class inheritance.

We'll look at the component system, which ASP.NET uses, in Chapter 6, and we'll also examine how to build reflective base classes in Chapter 3.

First, though, let's take a look at some of the underlying theory that underpins reflection. We'll be looking at:

❑ **Type Terminology**
   We'll just review some of the key terminology relating to types in .NET. Reflection, as a .NET API, uses the .NET terminology for a lot of things, rather than the VB.NET terms.

❑ **Binding**
How calls to methods are resolved in .NET. We'll see how VB.NET provides a partially dynamic binding system, and how reflection makes it truly dynamic.

❑ **Metadata**
Metadata is data that is compiled into .NET assemblies that describes the code in the assembly. We'll see that metadata is a prerequisite of reflection, and how .NET provides an extensible framework for metadata.

Type Terminology

Let's quickly go over some of the terminology we'll be using in this book. In dealing with reflection, we'll be dealing with types, and the words used to describe them and their members will be important. Here are the most important ones:

❑ **Type**
A type is a combination of a data structure and some code. There are two kinds of type: value types and reference types. Classes, arrays, and delegates are all reference types. Structures, primitives and enumerations are all value types.

❑ **Instance**
An instantiation of a particular type. An instance of a class is an `object`.

❑ **Type Member**
A type member is anything that is defined inside a type. Methods, fields, properties, events, and nested classes are all type members. Type members can be shared (known in .NET as a whole as static) members or instance members.

❑ **Method**
A container for code. In VB.NET, this is a `Sub` or a `Function`.

❑ **Field**
A container for data. Also called a member variable. Depending on whether it is shared or not, it may also be called a shared variable, or instance variable.

❑ **Signature**
The combination of a method's name and parameter list. Every method in a type has a unique signature.

When we say something is "type-safe", we mean it guarantees that no operations are attempted on an instance that are not permitted for an instance of that type. This guarantee is enforced at compile-time by the compiler, if `Option Strict` is turned on. If code is not type-safe, then the compiler can't guarantee this, and we have to check we haven't made any logic errors ourselves. If we have, then a runtime error may result.

Binding

We've talked briefly about late binding, but it's important, for understanding when exactly we need to use reflection, to consider it a little more formally. Binding is the process where a reference to a piece of code in our program is resolved to an actual program routine in memory. It's a fundamental part of the way programming languages operate, and in .NET, the way binding works enables such important object-oriented concepts as interfaces, polymorphism, and of course reflection.

Early (Static) Binding

In a basic procedural programming language, resolving a procedure call is not a complicated process at all. In such a language, we can define procedures, and then call them from other points in our code. So, if we have the following code (in an imaginary procedural language with VB.NET-like syntax):

```
Sub Foo()
  MsgBox("Foo called")
End Sub
```

And we have a call elsewhere in our code that looks like this:

```
Foo()
```

It should be obvious that when execution reaches this line, the code in the `Foo()` subroutine will be executed. The fact that this will happen is rigidly dictated by our code – no code elsewhere will interfere in the link between the call to `Foo()` and the code in the `Foo()` procedure being executed. This call is **statically bound**: it is fixed and unchanging.

If the code above were in a compiled language, then the compiler can do quite a lot of work to check that the procedure call is valid, and optimize the resulting code. If we misspelled the name of the procedure, or provided the wrong number of arguments, the compiler would be able to tell us that the call would definitely not work. The compiler also knows exactly where in memory the `Foo()` function will be loaded, and can compile the call to `Foo()` as a direct jump to that piece of memory. In fact, where the called function is short – as it is here – the compiler can just compile the code in the function inline where it's called, optimizing the code by eliminating an unnecessary jump.

Runtime Binding

Now, many procedural programming languages offer a second method for calling functions, via function pointers. This might (in our fictional language again) allow us to write code something like this:

```
PointerToProc = AddressOf Foo
PointerToProc()
```

Now things are a bit less static. At the point where the procedure is called – the `PointerToProc()` instruction – the exact code that is executed next is determined not by the instruction itself, but by the value previously assigned to `PointerToProc`. If the line setting the value of `PointerToProc` was inside, for example, a conditional construction such as an `If` block, the code that is executed by the call instruction will depend on the state of the program at the time that `If` block was executed. In this situation, the call to the procedure is **runtime bound**; which piece of code will be executed next is not fixed when the instruction is written, but will only be determined at runtime, depending on which instructions have been executed previously, and the state of the program.

You should note that the compiler can't make the assumptions it could make before with an early bound call. It knows where the procedure `Foo` is in memory, so can put this value into the variable `PointerToProc`, but it can't optimize the call to the procedure. The call will take a little longer at runtime, but the program can do many things that weren't possible in the completely static system.

Object-orientation

But as we know, .NET is not a procedural programming environment, and Visual Basic .NET is not a procedural programming language – we have to think in terms of objects and methods, not procedures.

Object-orientation makes binding more complicated, because instead of procedures, we have methods, and methods are defined in types (usually classes). When we define a type and give it a method, that method can be called on any object that is an instance of that type. So, say we have the following type definition (this is now proper VB.NET code, and the reason we've declared this method `Overridable` will become clear shortly):

```
Public Class Thing
    Public Overridable Sub Foo()
      MsgBox("Foo called on a Thing instance")
    End Sub
End Class
```

Then we can write code like the following:

```
Dim myThing As Thing
myThing = New Thing()
myThing.Foo()
```

As before, we're interested in how that call to Foo() is dispatched. What's going on this time? Well, the class definition containing a method declaration is really not all that different from the code that declared a procedure in our procedural language. Just like such a procedure, it will be loaded into memory at runtime, and sit at a particular location in memory. The challenge for the runtime engine is to work out that our call to myThing.Foo() needs to be translated into a jump to this point in memory. In the case shown here, it's not that complicated; the variable myThing contains an object of type Thing, so when the myThing.Foo() line is reached, it can be determined that the call is to the Foo() method on the Thing class. So far, it looks just like early binding. But that's not quite the case.

Since VB.NET is compiled, we should consider what the compiler will make of this. Obviously, the compiler is aware of the declared type of the myThing variable. So it would appear that the compiler can translate the call to Foo() as a jump to the Foo() method defined in the Thing class, just like it could in our early bound example. However, consider the following case:

```
Public Class SpecialThing
    Inherits Thing
  Public Overrides Sub Foo()
    MsgBox("Foo called on a SpecialThing instance")
  End Sub
End Class
```

We write another class that extends Thing. Instead of creating an instance of the Thing type in our other code, we create an instance of this new subclass:

```
Dim myThing As Thing
myThing = New SpecialThing()
myThing.Foo()
```

Now, recall that the compiler believes that the type of the myThing variable is Thing. But this doesn't preclude instances of subclasses of Thing being in that variable, as in this example. So the compiler can't assume that the call to myThing.Foo() needs to be sent to the Foo() subroutine in the Thing class. The actual type of the object in the variable will not be determined until runtime, since it will depend on the code that has executed previously. We refer to the declared type of a variable as its **compile-time type**, and the type of an object actually stored in a variable as its **runtime type**. So, the choice of which method is executed will be made at runtime, just like it was in the case of function pointers. So:

> **Calls to instance methods on .NET objects are normally runtime bound.**

We say 'normally' here because there are circumstances when the compiler can determine what the runtime type of a variable must be. This could be the case if the variable is of a type that is declared NotInheritable, for example. We also have to specify that this is only true of instance methods, because Shared methods (which aren't inherited) are always statically (early) bound. In fact, .NET's name for what VB.NET calls Shared type members is static, reflecting the fact that calls to them are statically bound.

So, whenever we make a statically bound call we are setting in stone in our code what will happen when the line we're writing is executed. The state of the program at the time the line is executed will have no effect on which code is executed next. A runtime bound call does not fix which code will execute alone; it depends on previous code putting the application in a particular state to specify exactly which code will be executed.

Late Binding

As we saw, as well as the compile-time checked early binding and runtime binding we've just seen, .NET allows late binding – both through VB.NET syntax with Option Strict off, and through reflection. The important question is, when exactly do we need to use late binding because runtime binding isn't adequate?

Let's consider the following problem: we have a variable, which is of type Object, which might contain a String or an Integer. If it contains a String, we want to display it on screen. If it contains an integer, we want to format it as a quantity of money, and display it on screen. How can we do that?

Here's one way we might attempt to code it:

```
Public Class Handler

    Public Overloads Sub Handle(ByVal s As String)
        Console.WriteLine(s)
    End Sub

    Public Overloads Sub Handle(ByVal i As Integer)
        Console.WriteLine(System.String.Format("{0:c}", i))
    End Sub

End Class

Module MainModule

    Public Sub Main()
        Dim a As New Handler()
        Dim o As Object
        o = "Hello"
        a.Handle(o)
```

```
      o = 1
      a.Handle(o)
   End Sub

End Module
```

With `Option Strict` off, this works just fine. But turn on `Option Strict`, and it doesn't compile, complaining that there's no overload of `Handle()` that takes an `Object`. We can add one, like this, and in fact it will reveal something interesting about how runtime and even late binding can sometimes be unpredictable:

```
Option Strict On

Public Class Handler

   Public Overloads Sub Handle(ByVal o As Object)
      Console.WriteLine("Can't Handle Object types")
   End Sub

   Public Overloads Sub Handle(ByVal s As String)
      Console.WriteLine(s)
   End Sub

   Public Overloads Sub Handle(ByVal i As Integer)
      Console.WriteLine(System.String.Format("{0:c}", i))
   End Sub

End Class

Module MainModule
   Public Sub Main()
      Dim a As New Handler()
      Dim o As Object
      o = "Hello"
      a.Handle(o)
      o = 1
      a.Handle(o)
   End Sub

End Module
```

So, if we call `Handles()` with an instance of `String` or `Integer` that's stored in a variable of type `Object`, what will happen? To put the question more formally – is it the runtime or compile-time type of the variable that's used to decide which overload to execute? Well, we know that the call to `Handle()` is runtime bound, in that the compiler does not decide which class's definition of the method to use at compile-time, in case a contains an instance of a subclass of `Handler`. So you might expect the overload resolution to be based on the runtime type of the object in o. That would be `String` or `Integer`, so the `Handle()` variation for the appropriate type should be executed. However, as you'll see if you run this code, the result is in fact that the `Object` variation is executed.

What actually happens is that .NET regards overloaded methods as completely different – as different as they would be if they had different names – so resolution of which variant of the method should be called happens at compile-time, in exactly the same way as method names are resolved at compile-time. The compiler uses the information it has available – the compile-time type of the o variable – to select which method will be called. At runtime, the decision is made about which class to look in for that method, but the overload resolution has already been solved, so the runtime type of the o variable is not queried.

What's particularly interesting is that if we turn Option Strict off on this code, the behavior isn't changed – the Object variant is always called. Supporting the default case, when someone passes in an object of an unsupported type, means that even VB.NET's late binding doesn't pass the object to the overload matching the runtime type of the variable.

In other words, we've just found a limit of the late binding provided by VB.NET. If we want to select a method that can accept a particular kind of object based on its *run-time* type, overloading doesn't provide a good mechanism for it, because overload resolution uses the compile-time type. In fact, there is no syntactic mechanism to reliably do what we want. What we need, in order to do this, is controllable late binding. Reflection provides this ability to take complete control at runtime of what code is executed.

Through the Reflection API, we can examine objects to determine their runtime type, look for methods which have a particular signature, and invoke those methods completely dynamically. But we should remember, the compiler will not be able to help us by checking that the types we are using are correct, and the language will not provide the convenient syntax for calling such methods. We'll have to write more complex code, which might introduce errors. To give you an idea of what we're talking about, the following invocation would replace the statically-overloaded method call above with a dynamic call to the most appropriate overload given the runtime type of the instance in the o variable:

```
a.GetType() _
    .GetMethod("OverloadedMethod", New Type() {o.GetType()}) _
    .Invoke(a, New Object() {o})
```

We'll be looking at exactly what all this means in the next few chapters. But all this coding overhead for a simple method call is, naturally, not the sort of thing you want to do every day, and we're certainly not advocating you use this technique to call all overloaded instance methods. There's a performance cost for all reflective API calls, and this code is more error-prone than the compile-time type-checked code we're used to writing. However, in those situations where the default binding behavior doesn't execute the code you want, you have no choice but to use reflection to get the job done. Hopefully you've now seen that even VB.NET's late binding doesn't solve all our problems.

Metadata

For a late bound system to work, certain information needs to be available at runtime, which in many languages wouldn't normally be retained after compilation. As we saw in our static bound examples, a compiler can replace a call to a static procedure or method with a jump directly to the location in memory where the method is located. There's no need, for example, for it to create a lookup table of procedure names, and compile each call as a lookup in this table. The actual name given to the procedure is irrelevant at runtime, and is typically discarded, just like variable names, original line numbers, and so on. The only reason for retaining this information might be for debugging, so that the programmer can be told which subroutine a crash occurred in. Similar arguments apply to the late bound examples – names, only meaningful to the programmer, not the computer – are generally discarded. But not in .NET.

In order to allow late binding of methods, we need to be able to access them by name at runtime. So, .NET stores the names of all methods as part of the metadata of every type, and it is possible to look up methods by name at runtime.

Similarly, in a statically bound language, where the compiler has been able to check that the arguments for every procedure call are all of the correct type, there is no need to retain at runtime the information about how many arguments, of what type, are required to call the function; every statically bound call has already been checked out, and will be correct; no calls are going to be constructed on the fly, so there is no need to perform a check at runtime.

But in a late bound system, we need this information so that we can correctly formulate method calls at runtime. So .NET also includes all the information about a method's signature in the compiled assembly.

All of this additional data stored in the assembly is called **metadata**. Metadata is data about the code in an assembly.

The Reflection API provides full functionality for examining the metadata in an assembly, associated with a type or type member. .NET also provides a mechanism for adding your own custom metadata to your code, through **attributes**, which can also be examined through reflection.

Accessing .NET Metadata

Reflection makes available all of the metadata stored in an assembly. .NET assemblies can tell us about all of the following things:

- ❑ The version of the assembly
- ❑ The modules contained in the assembly
- ❑ External assemblies referenced

❑   Classes, interfaces, and value types contained in the modules

❑   Class members: methods, properties, events, fields, constructors and enumerations

❑   Other resources used by the assembly (like image files)

There are, essentially, two "ways in" to the metadata used by the reflection system. Both routes lead us to exactly the same set of data. We can essentially go in from the top, or the bottom:

❑   From the bottom, we can start by obtaining metadata about the type of a particular object, then discover the assembly which contains it.

❑   From the top, we can start off with a reference to an assembly, and from there obtain assembly metadata, and discover what types it contains.

It helps to visualize the metadata in a hierarchical fashion as shown below:

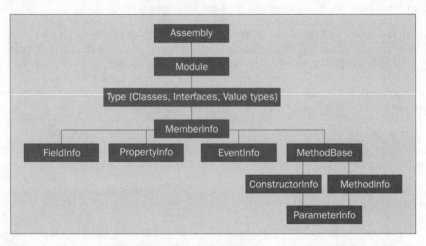

At the top of the hierarchy is the information about the assembly. The assembly metadata contains information about the assembly version, information about other assemblies that it accesses, other resources such as images, and so on.

At the next level of the hierarchy is information on modules. A module (in the sense used by .NET, rather than VB.NET) represents a DLL or EXE file, and it is possible to have more than one module in a single assembly. Modules contain a collection of types that represent classes, interfaces, or value types. Further down the metadata hierarchy, each type has a collection of members, like methods, constructors, properties, fields, and events.

Assembly, module, type and member metadata are all retrievable using classes from the System.Reflection namespace.

Assemblies, modules, and types are represented in reflection by instances of the `System.Reflection.Assembly`, `System.Reflection.Module` and `System.Type` classes respectively.

The `System.Reflection.MemberInfo` class is the base class for classes that contain class member metadata. Subclasses provide specific interfaces for accessing metadata relating to a particular kind of member. For example to retrieve information about a field, you obtain a `System.Reflection.FieldInfo` object. Similarly we have:

❑   `System.Reflection.MethodInfo`

❑   `System.Reflection.PropertyInfo`

❑   `System.Reflection.ConstructorInfo`

❑   `System.Reflection.EventInfo`

The `MethodInfo` and `ConstructorInfo` classes have some common characteristics and hence they are not directly derived form the `MemberInfo` class, but from a base class derived from `MemberInfo` called `System.Reflection.MethodBase`. The `MethodInfo` and `ConstructorInfo` classes can be further drilled down to one more level of the metadata hierarchy to retrieve information about its parameters, each of which can be represented by a `System.Reflection.ParameterInfo` object.

We'll be looking at all of these classes more closely in the next chapter.

Attributes

In addition to all the metadata that .NET relies upon to function, we can add our own metadata to any of these items in the metadata hierarchy, using **attributes**.

We can place attributes in many places in our code. They are compiled into our assemblies, and sit there waiting until some other code asks to see if they exist. .NET provides a massive number of attributes, which are used to control mechanisms such as serialization, remoting, web services, ASP.NET, and the behavior of components. In addition, we can define our own attributes. These are just the same as .NET's own attributes, and we can create systems that handle code using our custom attributes that are just as sophisticated as .NET's own offerings.

You can use attributes to provide labels and information about your types that will be visible to other code accessing them reflectively. If you have an automated testing program that checks all your code and meets the functional specification after you run a build, you could use an attribute to label and name a test method to be called on each type. A generic test harness could use this information to locate all the unit tests, and execute them, regardless of the precise methods provided on each class.

We'll look at attributes in a lot more depth in Chapter 5.

Reflection in .NET

In this book, we'll break down the kinds of tasks you can accomplish with reflection into the following sections:

Examining Objects

First of all, we'll look at what reflection can tell us about an object at runtime. We'll use reflection to show the names of an object's members, and the values of its fields. We'll examine the object's inheritance hierarchy, and determine if it can be safely cast to another type.

Manipulating Objects

We'll then look at how we can go about changing an object's state and calling methods reflectively. We'll see how a base class can provide services to its subclasses, and also examine when to use reflection and when not to. We'll particularly compare reflective access to delegates, and see which is appropriate and when.

Creating Objects

We'll look at how reflection can load assemblies and create new objects. We'll implement some of the classic creational Design Patterns, and show how reflection can effectively decouple an application's requirements from the module providing the service.

Summary

Reflection is a powerful late binding mechanism, which allows us to examine, modify and create objects at runtime. This means we can make use of information not available at compile-time to decide how our program should behave; this can include adding code later on in the form of extension modules.

We examined how .NET performs binding:

❑ Early (static) bound calls are fixed; if the call is executed, it will always lead to the same code being executed, regardless of the state of the program.

❑ Late bound calls are dynamic; they take account of the runtime type of objects.

❑ Polymorphism in .NET is handled through late binding of methods. Overloading, however, does not always use late binding.

❑ Reflection can be used to perform late binding using information ignored by static and runtime bound calls. You can use it to access overloaded methods based on the runtime type of parameters, and to access methods defined by complex protocols that can't be declared in an interface.

❑ Reflection can also bind types and assemblies dynamically.

Reflection relies on metadata being present at runtime to allow its dynamic binding. .NET provides a lot of metadata, and also allows programmers to add metadata in the form of attributes. They can even define their own custom attributes.

We examined the reasons reflection exists, and some cases where its use is necessary. In the rest of the book, we'll see it in action.

VB.NET

Reflection

Handbook

2

2

Examining Assemblies, Objects and Types

In the previous chapter we discussed the advantages of dynamic object binding, and learned that reflection is a mechanism we can use to perform dynamic binding from our programs. We saw how dynamic binding relies on metadata stored in assemblies, and then gave you an overview of .NET's Reflection API, and noted that the classes associated with it can be used to discover, examine, and manipulate the contents of an assembly by accessing its metadata.

What we didn't do was to start playing with some reflection classes, and using them in our programs. In this chapter we will begin to do exactly that. However, we are not going to try to run before we can walk, so we will be concentrating upon the passive use of reflection in this chapter: examining the types of objects, and searching through assemblies for classes, interfaces, and their members, and retrieving their metadata. We'll leave more active uses of reflection – invoking methods, manipulating properties, and instantiating objects via reflection – until later chapters.

We're going to start off the chapter by considering what metadata is available to the reflection system. This will mean looking at what exactly assemblies contain. We'll see why we would want to examine and retrieve assembly-level metadata, and how to do this using the classes of the Reflection API. We'll look at two classes that are particularly important to reflection – `System.Reflection.Assembly` – that contains information about an assembly, and `System.Type` – that contains information about the type (the class) of an object. We'll then see how to retrieve the type of an object as well as the metadata associated with its members. Finally we'll take a close look at the "info" classes used as containers for class member metadata.

Examining Assembly Metadata

Assemblies are the basic units of deployment; they contain a collection of types and resources. They can be considered as the building blocks of any .NET application. They are reusable, versionable, and self-describing, and stored as an EXE or a DLL file.

Assemblies also contain the infrastructure information that the CLR requires to understand the contents of the assembly and to enforce dependency and security rules defined by the application.

The contents of an assembly can be broadly classified into:

❑ The assembly manifest

❑ Type metadata (to store information about the members)

❑ Microsoft Intermediate Language (MSIL)

❑ A set of resources

The above contents can be grouped into a single file:

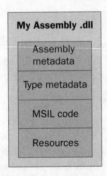

Alternatively, it can be in more than one file resulting in a **multifile** assembly:

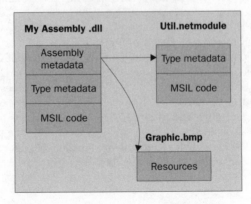

A multifile assembly is desirable when we want to combine modules written in different languages, or if we want to separate out code that is rarely used into separate modules, so that loading and execution of modules is faster.

Multifile assemblies are linked to their components using the information in the assembly's **manifest**, which contains the assembly metadata – a collection of data that describes how the elements in the assembly relate to each other. An assembly manifest contains all of the metadata needed to specify the assembly's version requirements and security identity, and to define the scope of the assembly and resolve references to resources and classes.

The assembly manifest can be stored in either a portable executable (PE) file (an EXE or DLL) with MSIL code or in a standalone PE file that contains only assembly manifest information. The metadata can be analyzed to retrieve the assembly name, version number, culture, and strong name information, which combined together, forms the assembly's identity. We'll look at assembly naming and loading in detail in Chapter 4, *Creating Objects*.

An assembly is represented in the Reflection class library by an object of type `System.Reflection.Assembly`. Let's take a look now at that class.

The Assembly Class

The `System.Reflection.Assembly` class provides access to all the metadata stored in the assembly's manifest. You can't obtain an `Assembly` object just by calling a constructor – you have to get one through one of the following mechanisms:

❑ Through a call to one of the `Assembly` class's shared `Get...()` methods:

- `GetAssembly(t As Type)`
- `GetCallingAssembly()`
- `GetEntryAssembly()`
- `GetExecutingAssembly()`

These return an `Assembly` object representing an already-loaded assembly. We'll look at them in detail in a moment.

❑ Through a call to one of the `Assembly` class's shared `Load...()` methods:

- `Load(...)`
- `LoadWithPartialName(...)`
- `LoadFrom(...)`

These methods are all overloaded. They load a specified assembly into memory, and return an `Assembly` object representing the loaded assembly. We'll look at these methods in Chapter 4.

❑ By querying the `Assembly` property of a `Type` object, to obtain an assembly object representing the assembly that defines that type. This returns exactly the same value as calling `Assembly.GetAssembly()` with the same type object.

❑ `AppDomain.GetAssemblies()` returns the assemblies loaded in a particular application domain. `AppDomain` also provides a number of events and other methods related to assembly loading.

The `Get...Assembly()` methods deserve a little more explanation, since they are the simplest way to get at an assembly that's already loaded into the .NET runtime.

❑ `Assembly.GetAssembly(t As Type)` returns the assembly in which the specified type is declared. As stated above, this is functionally equivalent to calling `t.GetAssembly()`.

❑ `Assembly.GetExecutingAssembly()` returns the assembly containing the currently executing code.

❑ `Assembly.GetCallingAssembly()` returns the assembly containing the method that called the currently executing method. This may be the same as the executing assembly, if the method was called by another method in the same assembly.

❑ `Assembly.GetEntryAssembly()` returns the assembly that contains the entry point for the current `AppDomain`. This will be the assembly containing the main form or `Main()` method of the application.

As you can see, you can find the current assembly, the assembly from which the currently executing code was called, or the assembly that was originally the entry point for the application in which your code is being run.

> *More detailed analysis of the current call stack (the list of methods which were called in order for execution to reach the current point in the program) can be performed using `System.Diagnostics.StackTrace`. This class will enable you to locate objects representing all of the executing methods, and from them you can work your way up through the reflection object model to locate the assemblies which contain them. This same process can be used to examine the assemblies which caused an exception to be thrown, since a `StackTrace` object can be obtained from an exception's `StackTrace` property.*

Having obtained an `Assembly` object, we have access to a number of methods and properties that give us information from the assembly's metadata. Here are the key properties:

Property	Type	Description
CodeBase	String	Full path of the assembly file, including the name of the assembly file.
EntryPoint	System.Reflection .MethodInfo	Gets an instance of MethodInfo that represents the method that would be called if this assembly was executed, or Nothing if the assembly is a DLL.
EscapedCodeBase	String	The CodeBase expressed as a clean URL, using standard URL escape characters for those which aren't valid in a URL (such as %20 for a space character).
Evidence	System.Security .Policy.Evidence	Evidence is used by the .NET security system to decide what permissions to grant to the code in an assembly. Objects of any type that are recognized by a security policy represent evidence. Common forms of evidence include signatures and location of origin of code, but can potentially be anything.
FullName	String	The full screen name of the assembly, including version, culture and strong name information.
GlobalAssemblyCache	Boolean	A value indicating if the assembly was loaded from the GAC or not.
Location	String	Location of the file containing the assembly manifest. Differs from CodeBase in that the CodeBase is always the location of a physical assembly, whereas a dynamically created assembly, which has no physical source file or manifest, has a blank Location and a CodeBase the same as the assembly that created it.

`Assembly` also provides the following methods:

Method	Description
CreateInstance()	Used to create an instance of a type defined in the assembly. We'll see this in use in Chapter 4.
GetCustomAttributes()	Gets any custom attributes defined on this assembly.
GetExportedTypes()	Returns an array of `Type` objects representing all the exported types in the assembly; exported types are types visible to COM applications.
GetFile()	Obtains a `FileStream` for a file referenced from the assembly manifest.
GetFiles()	Returns an array of `FileStream` objects connected to the files from the assembly manifest.
GetLoadedModules()	Returns an array of objects representing the modules in the assembly.
GetManifestResourceInfo()	Returns information about a specified resource.
GetManifestResourceNames()	Returns an array of strings representing the names of all the assembly's resources.
GetManifestResourceStream()	Returns a `Stream` for reading the specified resource.
GetModule()	Returns an object representing the specified module.
GetModules()	Gets all the modules that are part of this assembly. The first module in the returned array contains the assembly's manifest.
GetName()	Returns an `AssemblyName` object containing the assembly's name, version, culture and public key information.
GetReferencedAssemblies()	Returns an array of `AssemblyName` objects for all the assemblies referenced.
GetSatelliteAssembly()	A satellite assembly contains a set of resources for a specific culture. This method returns the satellite assembly for the specified culture.

Method	Description
GetType()	Returns a `Type` object for the type defined in the assembly with the specified name. Note that this overloads the `GetType()` no-arg method defined by `System.Object`, which returns the `Type` object representing the type of the object on which it's called.
GetTypes()	Returns an array of `Type` objects for all the types defined in the assembly.
IsDefined()	Returns a Boolean value indicating whether the assembly is decorated with an attribute of the specified type.
LoadModule()	Loads a specified module into the assembly.

Let's write a program that examines an assembly and retrieves the assembly metadata:

```
Imports System.Reflection
Module MainModule
  Sub Main()

    'Loads the assembly file
    Dim myAssembly As System.Reflection.Assembly = _
        System.Reflection.Assembly.GetExecutingAssembly()

    'Display the CodeBase
    Console.WriteLine("Code Base = {0}", myAssembly.CodeBase())
    Console.WriteLine()
    'Display the EntryPoint
    Console.WriteLine("Entry Point = {0}", _
                        myAssembly.EntryPoint.Name)
    Console.WriteLine()
    'Display the FullName
    Console.WriteLine("Full Name = {0}", myAssembly.FullName)
    Console.WriteLine()

    'Get the AssemblyName object of the assembly
    Dim asmName As AssemblyName = myAssembly.GetName
    'Display the simple name
    Console.WriteLine("Simple Name = {0}", AsmName.Name)
    Console.WriteLine()

    'Display the version information
    Dim asmVer As System.Version = asmName.Version
    Console.WriteLine("Major Version = {0}", AsmVer.Major)
    Console.WriteLine("Minor Version = {0}", AsmVer.Minor)
```

```
        Console.WriteLine("Build Version = {0}", AsmVer.Build)
        Console.WriteLine("Revision Version = {0}", AsmVer.Revision)
        Console.WriteLine()

        'Get an array of AssemblyName objects that represent the
        'assemblies referenced by this assembly
        Dim refAsmbs As AssemblyName() = _
            myAssembly.GetReferencedAssemblies
        Dim refAsmb As AssemblyName

        'Display the simple name of each referenced assembly
        System.Console.Write("Referenced Assemblies: ")
        For Each refAsmb In refAsmbs
          System.Console.Write("{0}, ", refAsmb.Name)
        Next
        Console.WriteLine()
        Console.WriteLine()

        'Get an array of Module objects that are contained in this
        'assembly
        Dim myModules As System.Reflection.Module() = _
            myAssembly.GetModules
        Dim myModule As System.Reflection.Module

        'Display the name of each module
        System.Console.Write("Modules Contained: ")
        For Each myModule In myModules
          System.Console.Write("{0}, ", myModule.Name)
        Next
        Console.WriteLine()
        Console.ReadLine()
    End Sub
End Module
```

If we look at the output from the program, we can see that the program examines the assembly associated with the program (I called the application AssemblyMeta):

```
Code Base = file:///C:/Documents and Settings/andrewpTEST/
My Documents/Visual Studio Projects/AssemblyMeta/bin/AssemblyMeta.exe

Entry Point = Main

Full Name = AssemblyMeta, Version=1.0.960.24866, Culture=neutral,
PublicKeyToken=null

Simple Name = AssemblyMeta

Major Version = 1
Minor Version = 0
Build Version = 960
Revision Version = 24866
```

```
Referenced Assemblies: mscorlib, Microsoft.VisualBasic, System,
System.Data, System.Xml,

Modules Contained: AssemblyMeta.exe,
```

Examining Type Metadata

The System.Type class is the gateway to all the reflection operations that we perform. Type is an abstract class that can be used to represent any type declaration:

- ❑ classes
- ❑ interfaces
- ❑ arrays
- ❑ value types
- ❑ enumerations
- ❑ pointers

Retrieving Types

Now that we know the kind of information that we can retrieve from a Type object, let's consider how we can obtain a Type object in the first place.

The GetType() Method and Operator

All classes inherit the GetType() method from System.Object. Therefore, if we call this method on *any* object, it will return a Type for that object:

```
Dim myType As System.Type = myObj.GetType()
```

If we want to get a Type object for a class we haven't instantiated, we can use a Shared overload of GetType() from the Type class:

```
Dim doubleType As System.Type = Type.GetType("System.Double")
```

As you can see, the Type.GetType() method requires that we pass the fully qualified name of a class along with the namespace as a String. This technique is generally used to get the type of a class that is contained in an external assembly.

You should note that, by default, any version of GetType() where we supply the name of the class as a parameter will perform a case-sensitive search for the type in question.

VB.NET also has an operator called `GetType`, which returns the type. This `GetType` operator is equivalent to the `typeof` operator in C#. It takes the defined classname (with namespaces if required) and returns the `Type` object; it is not necessary to instantiate the class in this case:

```
Dim doubleType As System.Type = GetType(System.Double)
```

The GetInterfaces() Method

The `Type.GetInterfaces()` can be used to obtain an array of `Type` objects representing the types of all of the interfaces implemented or inherited by the object we're interested in:

```
Dim myInterfaces As System.Type = myObj.GetInterfaces()
```

Module Methods

The `System.Reflection.Module` class (which represents a module for the purposes of reflection) contains several methods we can use to retrieve type information.

First, if we want to retrieve the `Type` object of one of the classes contained in this module we can use the `Module.GetType()` method. We need to pass a string containing the fully qualified name of the class:

```
Dim classType As System.Type = myModule.GetType("ClassName")
```

Since a module may contain more than one class definition, we may want to retrieve an array of `Type` objects representing all of the types defined in the module. To do this, call the `Module.GetTypes()` method. It is even possible to return an array of `Type` objects from a module that have been filtered according to some criteria, using the `FindTypes()` method (for more information about this method you should refer to the MSDN documentation).

Let's take a look at the members of the `Type` class.

Type Class Members

The members of `Type` can be used to retrieve information about a particular class, such as the constructors, methods, fields, properties, and events of a class, and even the module and the assembly in which the class is deployed. Here are some selected properties of the `Type` class:

Property	Type	Description
Name	String	Gets the name of the class. Note that only the simple name is returned, not the fully qualified name. For example, for the System.Reflection.Assembly class, the Name property would be Assembly.
FullName	String	Gets the fully qualified name of the class, including the namespace of the class.
Assembly	System.Reflection.Assembly	Retrieves the assembly in which the class is declared.
AssemblyQualifiedName	String	Gets the fully qualified name of the class (including the name of the assembly from which the class was loaded).
Attributes	TypeAttributes	This property gets an instance of a TypeAttributes enumeration object representing the attribute set of the class. Using TypeAttributes we can find out whether the class is an interface, or is an abstract class, whether the class is public or not, and whether the class is serializable, among other information.
IsClass	Boolean	Indicates whether the type is a class (not a value type or interface).
BaseType	System.Type	Gets the Type of the class from which the class directly inherits.
Module	System.Reflection.Module	Gets an instance of the Module (DLL or EXE) in which the class is defined.

And here are some methods of the `Type` class:

Method	Description
IsSubclassOf()	Returns a `Boolean` specifying whether the class derives from the class specified as an argument to the method.
IsInstanceOfType()	Returns a `Boolean` indicating whether the specified object (passed as a parameter to the method) is an instance of the current class.
GetMember()	Gets the specified member of the `Type` object as a `MemberInfo` object. The member is specified via a `String`.
GetMembers()	Gets the members of the `Type` object as an array of `MemberInfo` objects.
GetField()	Gets the specified field of the `Type` object as a `FieldInfo` object. The field is specified via a `String`.
GetFields()	Gets the fields of the `Type` object as an array of `FieldInfo` objects.
GetProperty()	Gets the specified property of the `Type` object as a `PropertyInfo` object. The property is specified via a `String`.
GetProperties()	Gets the properties of the `Type` object as an array of `PropertyInfo` objects.
GetMethod()	Gets the specified method of the `Type` object as a `MethodInfo` object. The property is specified via a `String`.
GetMethods()	Gets the methods of the `Type` object as an array of `MethodInfo` objects.
GetConstructor()	Gets the specified constructor of the `Type` object as a `ConstructorInfo` object. The property is specified via a `String`.
GetConstructors()	Gets the constructors of the `Type` object as an array of `ConstructorInfo` objects.
GetEvent()	Gets the specified public event of the `Type` object as a `EventInfo` object. The property is specified via a `String`.
GetEvents()	Gets the public events of the `Type` object as an array of `EventInfo` objects.

Let's create a simple console program that illustrates how to access type metadata:

```
Module Module1
  Sub Main()
    Dim t As Type = GetType(System.Object)
    Console.WriteLine("Type Name : {0}", t.Name)
    Console.WriteLine("Full Name : {0}", t.FullName)
    Console.WriteLine("Namespace : {0}", t.Namespace)
    Console.WriteLine("Assembly Name : {0}", _
                      t.Assembly.GetName.Name)
    Console.WriteLine("Module Name : {0}", t.Module.Name)
    Console.WriteLine("Assembly Qualified Name : {0}", _
                      t.AssemblyQualifiedName)
    Console.WriteLine("IsAbstract : {0}", t.IsAbstract)
    Console.WriteLine("IsArray : {0}", t.IsArray)
    Console.WriteLine("IsClass : {0}", t.IsClass)
    Console.WriteLine("IsCOMObject : {0}", t.IsCOMObject)
    Console.WriteLine("IsEnum : {0}", t.IsEnum)
    Console.WriteLine("IsInterface : {0}", t.IsInterface)
    Console.WriteLine("IsNotPublic : {0}", t.IsNotPublic)
    Console.WriteLine("IsPointer : {0}", t.IsPointer)
    Console.WriteLine("IsPrimitive : {0}", t.IsPrimitive)
    Console.WriteLine("IsPublic : {0}", t.IsPublic)
    Console.WriteLine("IsSealed : {0}", t.IsSealed)
    Console.WriteLine("IsSerializable : {0}", t.IsSerializable)
    Console.WriteLine("IsSpecialName : {0}", t.IsSpecialName)
    Console.WriteLine("IsValueType : {0}", t.IsValueType)
    Console.ReadLine()
  End Sub
End Module
```

As you can see from the output from the program, it examines the metadata for the System.Object type:

```
Type Name : Object
Full Name : System.Object
Namespace : System
Assembly Name : mscorlib
Module Name : mscorlib.dll
Assembly Qualified Name : System.Object, mscorlib, Version=1.0.3300.0,
Culture=neutral, PublicKeyToken=b77a5c561934e089
IsAbstract : False
IsArray : False
IsClass : True
IsCOMObject : False
IsEnum : False
IsInterface : False
IsNotPublic : False
IsPointer : False
IsPrimitive : False
IsPublic : True
IsSealed : False
IsSerializable : True
IsSpecialName : False
IsValueType : False
```

Examining Class Member Metadata

In the previous section we retrieved information about classes using reflection. Now we let's see how to access information about class members: fields, properties, methods, and events, as well as value types like enumerations.

To examine class member metadata you will need to retrieve one or more of the following "info" objects:

❑ `System.Reflection.MemberInfo` – base class for all member "info" classes

❑ `System.Reflection.FieldInfo` – represents metadata about a field

❑ `System.Reflection.PropertyInfo` – represents metadata about a property

❑ `System.Reflection.MethodInfo` – represents metadata about a method

❑ `System.Reflection.ConstructorInfo` – represents metadata about a constructor

❑ `System.Reflection.EventInfo` – represents metadata about an event

❑ `System.Reflection.ParameterInfo` – represents parameter metadata

You should note that while `FieldInfo`, `PropertyInfo`, and `EventInfo` all derive directly from `MemberInfo`, `MethodInfo` and `ConstructorInfo` derive from another subclass of `MemberInfo` called `MethodBase`, and `ParameterInfo` derives directly from `System.Object`.

One last thing worth noting before we dive into the "info" classes is that the `System.Type` class is itself a direct subclass of `MemberInfo`.

Here's the class hierarchy we've just discussed, but in an easy-to-digest graphical form:

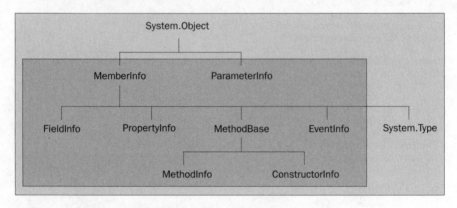

The Classes within the darker shaded box in the figure are within the System.Reflection namespace.

The MemberInfo Class

The MemberInfo class is an abstract base class, which provides an interface that is common to every member type. It contains some public properties that are inherited by all "info" classes:

Property	Type	Description
Name	String	Gets the name of the member
MemberType	System.Reflection .MemberTypes	Gets the member type (field, method, and so on)
DeclaringType	System.Type	Returns the Type of the class that declares this member
ReflectedType	System.Type	Returns the Type of the object that was used to obtain this MemberInfo instance

The System.Reflection.MemberTypes enumeration can take the following values:

- ❏ Field
- ❏ Property
- ❏ Method
- ❏ Constructor
- ❏ Event
- ❏ NestedType (specifies a nested type, that extends MethodInfo)
- ❏ TypeInfo (specifies the member is a type)
- ❏ Custom (specifies a custom member type)
- ❏ All (specifies all member types)

The MemberInfo class can be retrieved from a Type object using either the GetMember() or GetMembers(). The GetMember() method takes the name of the member as a parameter and returns a MemberInfo object. The GetMembers() method returns an array of MemberInfo objects. By default, if you do not provide any parameters to the above methods, they retrieve only the public members.

The BindingFlags Enumeration

Both the GetMember() and the GetMembers() methods (and many other methods that we will encounter as we use reflection) have overloaded versions that take a System.Reflection.BindingFlags enumeration value as a parameter. This enumeration specifies flags that control binding and the way in which the search for members and types is conducted by reflection. It is often used to filter and retrieve only those members that are of interest to the application. Here are some the most commonly used BindingFlag flag values:

Enumeration Value	Description
CreateInstance	Specifies that an instance of the specified type should be created
DeclaredOnly	Specifies that inherited members should be ignored
Default	Specifies no binding flag
GetField	Specifies that the value of the specified field should be returned
GetProperty	Specifies that the value of the specified property should be returned
InvokeMethod	Specifies that a particular method (not a constructor) is to be invoked
Public / NonPublic	Specifies that only public/non-public members are to be returned
SetField	Specifies that the value of the specified field should be set
SetProperty	Specifies that the value of the specified property should be set
Static / Instance	Specifies that only shared/instance members are to be returned

BindingTypes is an enumeration type that allows a bitwise combination of its member values, so we can specify more than one of the above conditions at once.

Let's have a few snippets of code to illustrate the use of GetMembers() and BindingFlags. If we want to retrieve only those members of a Type object myType that are static and public, we can use the following syntax:

```
myType.GetMembers(Reflection.BindingFlags.Static _
                  Or Reflection.BindingFlags.Public)
```

Or if we want to retrieve only those members that are non-public and non-static we can use:

```
myType.GetMembers(Reflection.BindingFlags.NonPublic _
                    Or Reflection.BindingFlags.Instance)
```

Note that you must specify either BindingFlags.Instance or
BindingFlags.Static, and either BindingFlags.Public or
BindingFlags.NonPublic in order to get a return.

In both cases, the return we get is an array of MemberInfo objects that fulfill the
conditions of the member search.

The following program retrieves the members of a class (called Employee) and
displays their names and types:

```
Imports System.Reflection
Module Module1

  Sub Main()
    Dim typ As System.Type = GetType(Employee)
    Dim membs As MemberInfo() = _
        typ.GetMembers(BindingFlags.Public Or _
        BindingFlags.NonPublic Or _
        BindingFlags.Static Or _
        BindingFlags.Instance Or _
        BindingFlags.DeclaredOnly)
    Dim memb As MemberInfo
    Console.WriteLine("MEMBER NAME".PadRight(20) + "MEMBER TYPE")
    Console.WriteLine()
    For Each memb In membs
      Dim nameStr As String = (memb.Name).PadRight(20)
      Console.WriteLine("{0}" + "{1}", nameStr, memb.MemberType)
    Next
    Console.ReadLine()
  End Sub

  Public Class Employee
    Private EmpName As String
    Private DoB As Date

    Public Function GetAge() As Integer
    End Function

    Private Sub ComputeOvertime()
    End Sub

    Private Property DateOfBirth() As Date
      Get
        Return DoB
      End Get
      Set(ByVal Value As Date)
        DoB = Value
```

```
          End Set
       End Property

       Public Property Name() As String
          Get
             Return EmpName
          End Get
          Set(ByVal Value As String)
             EmpName = Value
          End Set
       End Property
    End Class

 End Module
```

Here's what we expect to see from the program:

```
MEMBER NAME          MEMBER TYPE

EmpName              Field
DoB                  Field
GetAge               Method
ComputeOvertime      Method
get_DateOfBirth      Method
set_DateOfBirth      Method
get_Name             Method
set_Name             Method
.ctor                Constructor
DateOfBirth          Property
Name                 Property
```

The FieldInfo Class

This class provides access to field metadata. Let's have a look at some of its most important properties and methods (remember that since FieldInfo inherits from MemberInfo, it inherits its members too). Here are the properties:

Property	Type	Description
Name	String	Gets the name of this field
IsPrivate	Boolean	Gets a value indicating whether the field is private
IsPublic	Boolean	Gets a value indicating whether the field is public
IsStatic	Boolean	Gets a value indicating whether the field is static

Property	Type	Description
IsAssembly	Boolean	Returns a value indicating whether this field has Assembly level visibility (it can be accessed only from members inside the same assembly)
IsFamily	Boolean	Returns a value indicating whether this field has Family level visibility (it can be accessed only from members in the same class or from subclasses of that class)
IsFamilyAndAssembly	Boolean	Returns a value indicating whether this field has both Family and Assembly level visibility
IsFamilyOrAssembly	Boolean	Returns a value indicating whether this field has either Family Or Assembly level visibility
IsInitOnly	Boolean	Gets a value showing whether the field can only be set in the body of the constructor
IsLiteral	Boolean	Gets a value showing whether the value is written at compile time and cannot be changed
IsNotSerialized	Boolean	Gets a value indicating whether this field has the NotSerialized attribute

Here are the methods:

Method	Description
FieldType()	Returns a Type object that corresponds to the type of the field.
GetValue()	Retrieves the value of the field. It takes an Object as a parameter, which should be an instance of the class in which it is declared or must be an instance of a class that inherits the field. It returns an Object type, which contains the appropriate subclass.
SetValue()	Used to assign a new value to the field. You need to pass two Object parameters to the method: an instance of the class in which the field is declared (or an instance of a class that inherits the field), and the new value of the field.

You should note that as long as code in the assembly is trusted, there is no problem with retrieving or modifying the values of private fields using GetValue() and SetValue().

FieldInfo can be retrieved from any Type object using one of the two methods GetField() and GetFields(). The GetFields() method returns an array of FieldInfo objects each corresponding to one field inside the class. The GetField() method returns one FieldInfo object corresponding to the name of the field which is passed as a String parameter. Both methods can also take the BindingFlags enumeration, although if no BindingFlags enumeration values are passed to the methods, they will retrieve only the public fields.

For example, if we want to retrieve only private and instance fields from a Type object myType we use the following syntax:

```
myType.GetFields(BindingFlags.NonPublic Or BindingFlags.Instance)
```

In the following program, we use the FieldInfo class to retrieve metadata about the field NaN of the System.Double class:

```
Imports System.Reflection
Module Module1
    Sub Main()
        Dim t As Type = GetType(System.Double)
        Dim myFieldInfo As FieldInfo = t.GetField("NaN")
        Console.WriteLine("FIELD NAME: {0}", myFieldInfo.Name)
Console.WriteLine()
        Console.WriteLine("Member type: {0}", _
                          myFieldInfo.MemberType.ToString)
        Console.WriteLine("Class declared in: {0}", _
                          myFieldInfo.DeclaringType.Name)
        Console.WriteLine("Field Type: {0}", _
                          myFieldInfo.FieldType.Name)
        Dim x As Double = 5.0
        Console.WriteLine("Field Value: {0}", myFieldInfo.GetValue(x))
        Console.WriteLine("Has Assembly Level Visibility: {0}", _
                          myFieldInfo.IsAssembly)
        Console.WriteLine("Has Family Level Visibility: {0}", _
                          myFieldInfo.IsFamily)
        Console.WriteLine("Has FamilyAndAssembly Level Visibility: {0}", _
                          myFieldInfo.IsFamilyAndAssembly)
        Console.WriteLine("Has FamilyOrAssembly Level Visibility: {0}", _
                          myFieldInfo.IsFamilyOrAssembly)
        Console.WriteLine("IsInitOnly: {0}", myFieldInfo.IsInitOnly)
        Console.WriteLine("IsLiteral: {0}", myFieldInfo.IsLiteral)
        Console.WriteLine("IsNotSerialized: {0}", _
            myFieldInfo.IsNotSerialized)
        Console.WriteLine("IsPrivate: {0}", myFieldInfo.IsPrivate)
        Console.WriteLine("IsPublic: {0}", myFieldInfo.IsPublic)
        Console.WriteLine("IsStatic: {0}", myFieldInfo.IsStatic)
        Console.ReadLine()
    End Sub
End Module
```

Here's what we see when the program is run:

```
FIELD NAME: NaN

Member type: Field
Class declared in: Double
Field Type: Double
Field Value: NaN
Has Assembly Level Visibility: False
Has Family Level Visibility: False
Has FamilyAndAssembly Level Visibility: False
Has FamilyOrAssembly Level Visibility: False
IsInitOnly: False
IsLiteral: True
IsNotSerialized: False
IsPrivate: False
IsPublic: True
IsStatic: True
```

The PropertyInfo Class

The `PropertyInfo` class provides access to property metadata. Here are the relevant properties of the class:

Property	Type	Description
Name	String	Returns the name of the property as a `String`
PropertyType	System.Type	Returns a `Type` object that represents the type of the property field
CanRead	Boolean	Returns a `Boolean` stating if the property can be read
CanWrite	Boolean	Returns a `Boolean` stating if the property can be written to

Here are the relevant methods of the `PropertyInfo` class:

Method	Description
GetValue()	Retrieves the value of the property as an `Object` (takes the same arguments as `FieldInfo.GetValue()`)
SetValue()	Assigns a new value to the property (requires the same arguments as `FieldInfo.SetValue()`)
GetGetMethod()	Returns a `MethodInfo` object that contains information about the `Get` accessor of the property
GetSetMethod()	Returns a `MethodInfo` object that contains information about the `Set` accessor of the property

Similar to how we retrieved field metadata for a class in the previous section, it is possible to retrieve `PropertyInfo` objects for a class using the `Type.GetProperties()` or the `Type.GetProperty()` methods. The `GetProperty()` method is used to retrieve information about a single property of the class, so you need to supply the name of the property as `String` argument to the method. The `GetProperties()` method returns all the public properties of the class if you do not pass any `BindingFlags` parameters.

Let's write a program that loads an external assembly file (`System.dll`) and scans through all the members of the assembly to find non-abstract classes. It then delves into those non-abstract classes and retrieves only those properties that are static and non-public. We then examine each of them and display only those properties whose values can be read but cannot be modified:

```
Imports System.Reflection
Module Module1
  Sub Main()
    Dim strAsmbName As String = _
      "C:\\WINNT\\Microsoft.NET\\Framework\\v1.0.3705\\System.dll"
    Dim objAssembly As System.Reflection.Assembly = _
      System.Reflection.Assembly.LoadFrom(strAsmbName)

    Dim typs As System.Type() = objAssembly.GetTypes
    Dim typ As System.Type
    Dim i As Integer = 0
    Console.WriteLine("PROPERTY NAME".PadRight(35) + "PROPERTY TYPE")
    Console.WriteLine()
    For Each typ In typs
      If typ.IsClass And Not typ.IsAbstract Then
        Dim props As PropertyInfo() = _
            typ.GetProperties(BindingFlags.NonPublic Or _
            BindingFlags.Static)
        Dim prop As PropertyInfo
        For Each prop In props
          If prop.CanRead And Not prop.CanWrite Then
            i += 1
            Dim strName As String = (prop.Name).PadRight(35)
            Console.WriteLine("{0}" + "{1}", strName, _
                prop.PropertyType.Name)
          End If

        Next
      End If
    Next
    Console.WriteLine()
    Console.WriteLine("Total Properties Displayed = {0}", i)
    Console.ReadLine()
  End Sub
End Module
```

In the above program I am loading the System.dll *assembly file from the directory where the .NET Framework is installed in my system* (C:\WINNT\Microsoft.NET\Framework\v1.0.3705\System.dll). *You may have to change the path in code to point to the correct location of the file in your system.*

Here's what we see if we run the program:

```
PROPERTY NAME                            PROPERTY TYPE

Empty                                    RegexPrefix
IntrinsicTypeConverters                  Hashtable
UiPermission                             Boolean
UserInteractive                          Boolean
SwitchSettings                           IDictionary
AssertUIEnabled                          Boolean
LogFileName                              String
AutoFlush                                Boolean
IndentSize                               Int32
PerfomanceCountersFileMappingSize        Int32
HashCodeProvider                         IHashCodeProvider
Comparer                                 IComparer
UserInteractive                          Boolean
LocalHost                                IPHostEntry
ConfigTable                              Hashtable
ModuleList                               ArrayList
SetConfigurationSystemInProgress         Boolean
MsCorLibDirectory                        String
MachineConfigurationFilePath             String
AppConfigPath                            Uri
ComputerName                             String
DllPath                                  String
IniFilePath                              String
SymbolFilePath                           String
FileView                                 FileMapping
CurrentEnvironment                       Int32

Total Properties Displayed = 26
```

The MethodBase Class

The MethodBase class is an abstract class, which is inherited from the MemberInfo class. It provides information about methods and constructors. The MethodInfo and ConstructorInfo classes are inherited from the MethodBase class.

The MethodBase class declares certain methods and properties that are inherited in the ConstructorInfo and MethodInfo classes. Here are the properties:

Property	Type	Description
IsConstructor	Boolean	Gets a value indicating whether the method is a constructor
IsAbstract	Boolean	Returns a value indicating whether the method must be overridden
IsPrivate	Boolean	Gets a value indicating whether this member is private
IsPublic	Boolean	Gets a value indicating whether this is a public method
IsStatic	Boolean	Gets a value indicating whether the method is shared
IsVirtual	Boolean	Gets a value indicating whether the method is overridable
IsFamily	Boolean	This property is True if the method is accessible only by the members of the class and its derived classes
IsFamilyAndAssembly	Boolean	This property is True if the method is accessible only by the members of the class and its derived classes that are in the same assembly
IsFamilyOrAssembly	Boolean	This property is True if the method is accessible only by the members of the class and its derived classes, and also if it can be accessed by other classes in the same assembly
IsFinal	Boolean	This property is True if the method is Final, which means that this method cannot be overridden

And here are the methods:

Method	Description
GetParameters()	When overridden in a subclass, returns the parameters of the specified method or constructor as ParameterInfo objects
Invoke()	Invokes the method or constructor. We need to pass this method an array containing the parameters for the method/constructor we want to invoke. If we want to invoke a method, we need to pass the instance that created that method too

The MethodInfo Class

The MethodInfo class is used to access the method metadata. Since it is a subclass of MethodBase, it inherits the properties of that class, although it also adds a few other properties and methods of its own, including the ReturnType property. This property retrieves the return type of the method as a Type object.

The MethodInfo class can be obtained by invoking the GetMethod() or GetMethods() methods on a Type object.

Just as in the case of GetProperty() and the GetProperties() methods, the GetMethod() and the GetMethods() methods of the Type class are used depending on whether we want to examine a particular method whose name is known in advance (and we supply as a String argument), or whether we want to examine all the methods in a class which match a particular criteria using the BindingFlags parameters.

The following program illustrates how to access the method metadata that we discussed above, for a method called ComputeOvertime() of the Employee class:

```
Imports System.Reflection
Module Module1

  Sub Main()
    Dim typ As System.Type = GetType(Employee)
    Dim myMethod As MethodInfo = typ.GetMethod("ComputeOvertime", _
       BindingFlags.NonPublic Or BindingFlags.Instance _
       Or BindingFlags.Static Or BindingFlags.Public)
    Console.WriteLine("Member Type: {0}", myMethod.MemberType)
    Console.WriteLine("Method Name: {0}", myMethod.Name)
    Console.WriteLine("Method declared in Class : {0}", _
       myMethod.DeclaringType.Name)
    Console.WriteLine("IsAbstract : {0}", myMethod.IsAbstract)
    Console.WriteLine( _
      "Can be called from other classes in the same assembly: {0}", _
      myMethod.IsAssembly)
    Console.WriteLine("IsConstructor: {0}", myMethod.IsConstructor)
    Console.WriteLine("IsFinal: {0}", myMethod.IsFinal)
    Console.WriteLine("IsPrivate: {0}", myMethod.IsPrivate)
    Console.WriteLine("IsPublic: {0}", myMethod.IsPublic)
    Console.WriteLine("IsStatic: {0}", myMethod.IsStatic)
    Console.WriteLine("IsVirtual: {0}", myMethod.IsVirtual)
    Console.WriteLine("Return type: {0}", myMethod.ReturnType.Name)
    Console.ReadLine()
  End Sub

  Public Class Employee
    Private Shared Function ComputeOvertime() As Double

    End Function
  End Class

End Module
```

When the program is run, here's what is displayed in the console:

```
Member Type: Method
Method Name: ComputeOvertime
Method declared in Class : Employee
IsAbstract : False
Can be called from other classes in the same assembly: False
IsConstructor: False
IsFinal: False
IsPrivate: True
IsPublic: False
IsStatic: True
IsVirtual: False
Return type: Double
```

The ConstructorInfo Class

The ConstructorInfo class provides access to constructor metadata. The members of the ConstructorInfo class are similar to the members of the MethodInfo class since both are derived from the MethodBase class.

A ConstructorInfo object can be retrieved by invoking the GetConstructors() or GetConstructor() methods on the Type object associated with a class, in the same way as we use GetMethod() and GetMethods() to retrieve MethodInfo objects.

Let us write a program that will retrieve all the constructors of our Employee class:

```
Imports System.Reflection
Module Module1

  Sub Main()
    Dim typ As System.Type = GetType(Employee)
    Dim myMethod As ConstructorInfo = typ.GetConstructors()(0)

    Console.WriteLine("Member Type: {0}", myMethod.MemberType)
    Console.WriteLine("Constructor Name: {0}", _
        myMethod.ConstructorName)
    Console.WriteLine("Constructor declared in Class : {0}", _
        myMethod.DeclaringType.Name)
    Console.WriteLine("IsAbstract : {0}", myMethod.IsAbstract)
    Console.WriteLine( _
        "Can be called from other classes in the same assembly: {0}", _
        myMethod.IsAssembly)
    Console.WriteLine("IsConstructor: {0}", _
        myMethod.IsConstructor)
    Console.WriteLine("IsFinal: {0}", myMethod.IsFinal)
    Console.WriteLine("IsPrivate: {0}", myMethod.IsPrivate)
    Console.WriteLine("IsPublic: {0}", myMethod.IsPublic)
    Console.WriteLine("IsStatic: {0}", myMethod.IsStatic)
```

```
        Console.WriteLine("IsVirtual: {0}", myMethod.IsVirtual)
        Console.ReadLine()
    End Sub

    Public Class Employee
        Private Shared Function ComputeOvertime() As Double

        End Function
    End Class

End Module
```

Here's what we see when we execute the program. Since we haven't defined a constructor for the Employee class explicitly, the constructor metadata retrieved is for the default constructor (.ctor):

```
Member Type: Constructor
Constructor Name: .ctor
Constructor declared in Class : Employee
IsAbstract : False
Can be called from other classes in the same assembly: False
IsConstructor: True
IsFinal: False
IsPrivate: False
IsPublic: True
IsStatic: False
IsVirtual: False
```

The EventInfo Class

The EventInfo class is used to access event metadata. It declares the following properties:

Property	Type	Description
IsMulticast	Boolean	Returns True if the event is part of a multicast delegate
EventHandlerType	System.Type	Returns the Type of the event handler delegate associated with this event

And the following methods:

Method	Description
GetAddMethod()	Returns the method used to add an event handler delegate to the event source as a MethodInfo object
GetRaiseMethod()	Returns the method that is called when the event is raised as a MethodInfo object
GetRemoveMethod()	Returns the method used to remove an event handler delegate from the event source as a MethodInfo object
AddEventHandler()	Adds an event handler to an event source (you need to supply two arguments for this: an Object representing the event source, and a delegate encapsulating the event handler)
RemoveEventHandler()	Removes an event handler from an event source (requires the same arguments as AddEventHandler())

The EventInfo class can be obtained by invoking the GetEvent() or GetEvents() methods on the Type object of a class. Similar to other info classes, we can specify the event we are interested in as a String and pass it to GetEvent(), or we can retrieve an array of EventInfo objects from GetEvents().

In the following program, we retrieve metadata about the events in our Employee class:

```
Imports System.Reflection
Module Module1

  Sub Main()
    Dim x As Employee = New Employee()
    Dim typ As System.Type = x.GetType
    Dim myEvent As EventInfo = typ.GetEvent("AnEvent")
    Console.WriteLine("Event Name: {0}", myEvent.Name)
    Console.WriteLine("Declared in Class: {0}", _
        myEvent.DeclaringType.Name)
    Console.WriteLine("GetAddMethod: {0}", myEvent.GetAddMethod.Name)
    Console.WriteLine("GetRemoveMethod: {0}", _
        myEvent.GetRemoveMethod.Name)
    Console.WriteLine("IsMulticast: {0}", myEvent.IsMulticast)
    Console.WriteLine("Member Type: {0}", myEvent.MemberType.ToString)
    Console.ReadLine()
    End Sub

End Module

Public Class Employee
    Public Event AnEvent(ByVal EventNumber As Integer)
End Class
```

As you can see the from the output, the program tells us that there is just one event, called AnEvent, defined in the Employee class:

```
Event Name: AnEvent
Declared in Class: Employee
GetAddMethod: add_AnEvent
GetRemoveMethod: remove_AnEvent
IsMulticast: True
Member Type: Event
```

The ParameterInfo Class

The ParameterInfo class allows access to event metadata. As mentioned earlier, it is not derived from MemberInfo, but directly from System.Object.

The ParameterInfo class has the following properties:

Property	Type	Description
Attributes	System.Reflection .ParameterAttributes	Gets the attributes for this parameter as a ParameterAttributes enumeration
DefaultValue	Boolean	Gets a value indicating the default value of the parameter
IsRetval	Boolean	Gets a value indicating whether this is a Retval parameter
IsIn	Boolean	True, if this is used as an input parameter
IsOut	Boolean	True, if this is used as an output parameter
Position	Integer	This property returns the position of the parameter in the signature of the method, as an Integer
IsOptional	Boolean	Returns True if this parameter is an optional parameter
ParameterType	System.Type	This returns the type of the parameter like String, Integer, Object, Employee and so on

It is possible to retrieve information about parameters of a method or a constructor by invoking the `GetParameters()` method on `ConstructorInfo` or `MethodInfo` objects. The `GetParameters()` method does not require any parameters and returns an array of `ParameterInfo` objects.

Let's write a program that illustrates the use of `ParameterInfo`. This program retrieves the parameter metadata for the method `ComputeOvertime()` of the class `Employee`:

```vb
Imports System.Reflection
Module Module1

    Sub Main()
        Dim typ As System.Type = GetType(Employee)
        Dim myMethod As MethodInfo = typ.GetMethod("ComputeOvertime", _
            BindingFlags.Static Or BindingFlags.Public)
        Dim myParameters As ParameterInfo() = myMethod.GetParameters
        Dim myParameter As ParameterInfo
        Console.WriteLine("Function Name : {0}", myMethod.Name)
        Console.WriteLine("Number of Parameters : {0}", _
            myParameters.Length)
        Console.WriteLine()
        Dim i As Integer = 0
        For Each myParameter In myParameters
          i += 1
          Console.WriteLine("Parameter{0}", i)
          Console.WriteLine("Parameter Name: {0}", myParameter.Name())
          Console.WriteLine("Parameter Type: {0}", _
              myParameter.ParameterType.Name)
          Console.WriteLine("Function Name: {0}", myParameter.Member.Name)
          Console.WriteLine("Parameter Position: {0}", _
              myParameter.Position)
          Console.WriteLine("Is Input Parameter: {0}", myParameter.IsIn)
          Console.WriteLine("Is Parameter Optional: {0}", _
              myParameter.IsOptional)
          Console.WriteLine("Is Output Parameter: {0}", myParameter.IsOut)
          Console.WriteLine("Is Return Value Parameter: {0}", _
              myParameter.IsRetval)
          Console.WriteLine()
        Next
        Console.ReadLine()
    End Sub

    Public Class Employee
        Public Shared Function ComputeOvertime( _
            ByVal EmployeeNo As String, ByVal FromDate As Date, _
            ByVal ToDate As Date) As Double

        End Function
    End Class

End Module
```

Here's what we see when the program is run. As you can see, the program reports that the `ComputeOvertime()` method has three parameters:

```
Function Name : ComputeOvertime
Number of Parameters : 3

Parameter1
Parameter Name: EmployeeNo
Parameter Type: String
Function Name: ComputeOvertime
Parameter Position: 0
Is Input Parameter: False
Is Parameter Optional: False
Is Output Parameter: False
Is Return Value Parameter: False

Parameter2
Parameter Name: FromDate
Parameter Type: DateTime
Function Name: ComputeOvertime
Parameter Position: 1
Is Input Parameter: False
Is Parameter Optional: False
Is Output Parameter: False
Is Return Value Parameter: False

Parameter3
Parameter Name: ToDate
Parameter Type: DateTime
Function Name: ComputeOvertime
Parameter Position: 2
Is Input Parameter: False
Is Parameter Optional: False
Is Output Parameter: False
Is Return Value Parameter: False
```

Summary

In this chapter we considered why we would want to examine assembly metadata, and then showed you how to do so using the classes of the Reflection API.

We took a close look at the `System.Type` class, often considered to be the gateway to most of the activities you'll want to do using reflection. We saw that the `Type` class represents a type, and contains data such as the name of the type, the attributes associated with it, the assembly that it is located in, and so on. We also noted that you could retrieve the `Type` associated with any object by calling the `GetType()` method.

Then we considered how to dive a little deeper and examine the metadata associated with the members of a particular type. We saw that each kind of member – fields, properties, methods, constructors, and events – has an "info" class associated with it:

- ❏ `FieldInfo`
- ❏ `PropertyInfo`
- ❏ `MethodInfo`
- ❏ `ConstructorInfo`
- ❏ `EventInfo`

We can call the properties and methods of these classes to retrieve metadata about the class members they are associated with. Method parameters also have an `info` class associated with them – `ParameterInfo`.

To retrieve these `info` classes, we need to call the `Get` methods associated with the class member we're interested in – such as `GetProperty()` or `GetMethod()` – on the object that contains the member. We also noted that we can control the metadata returned to us by these methods using the `BindingFlags` enumeration.

You should note that we focused upon the passive use of reflection in this chapter. We examined the contents of assemblies using reflection, but we didn't attempt to call any members or modify any class data. In the next chapter we will look at using reflection in this more active way.

VB.NET

Reflection

Handbook

3

3

Using Objects

In the last chapter, we started looking at how to use the Reflection API in VB.NET code, specifically to retrieve the metadata from an assembly. This was a passive use of reflection: we didn't actually create or use any objects from the assembly. In this section, we will begin to see how we can use reflection in a more active way, to:

❑ Dynamically invoke and access instantiated objects

❑ Dynamically modify object fields

❑ Dynamically modify object properties

And after we have shown you how to do this in our code, we'll consider situations that are best tackled using other approaches (such as using delegates).

However, let's first take a step back and consider why we would want to use reflection to dynamically invoke or manipulate methods, fields and properties.

Why Invoke Members Using Reflection?

There are many applications around that make use of reflection in a far more active way than simply browsing through the metadata of a class or assembly. For example, the Visual Studio .NET IDE itself comes equipped with programming tools such as Intellisense, a Class Browser, a Property viewer, a Debugger, or even the ToolBox, which all use reflection to do many things that wouldn't otherwise be possible. On the surface these tools might seem plain and simple, but underneath they're busy discovering types, analyzing them, instantiating objects, accessing and invoking methods dynamically.

Let's consider a situation when you might want to invoke members reflectively. Say you had lots of user interface form windows that each had a host of controls: textboxes, listboxes, radio controls, and so on. Since you are dealing with user input, you also want to implement some kind of mechanism to check that these controls have been filled in or selected correctly by the user before your application uses the data from the user interface.

Now, you could create user input checking routines for each form. However, a simpler approach would be to create an input-checking method for each type of control that might be used on the form. Then we could create a generic routine that would be invoked for any form, that would use reflection to discover the types of controls on the form, and dynamically invoke the correct input-checking method. This technique would not only be simpler, but would enhance the extensibility of the system because we could easily add new forms to our application without needing to create a specific routine to handle input-checking. And if the form contained a control we haven't dealt with before, we just create a new input-checking routine for that control, which can be reused in other new forms.

A different scenario where dynamic method invocation could be useful might arise if you utilized existing COM Servers into your application. Briefly, COM Servers cannot be directly instantiated apparently because they have no manifest information. You need to have a wrapper class (also known as a proxy or an adapter) that allows you to be able to use your COM logic, but even then, your application has to be aware of this at compile time (early binding), since you need the component's type library to be able to create the wrapper class. But suppose this type library is inaccessible. The only way to invoke the component's methods is to use reflection to find and invoke the methods dynamically.

There really are endless possibilities and situations where you'd consider dynamic invocation through reflection. We'll move on through the chapter and see how we can use these capabilities and implement them in real-world situations.

Invoking Members Dynamically

Previously we've seen how the "info" classes (`MethodInfo`, `PropertyInfo`, and so on) can be used for determining and retrieving metadata associated with an object. However, these classes can do more than just that. We're now going to look at how these classes from the Reflection API allow us to dynamically invoke members of an object, be it invoking methods, retrieving or modifying properties, or fields. We finish the section by taking a close look at the `Type.InvokeMember()` method, that can do this too.

Invoking Class Members Using the Info Classes

We've instantiated a type and located the correct method; next, we want to invoke and access object members (be it methods, properties, or fields) at runtime. There are mainly two different ways to perform dynamic invocation. The first is through the info classes from the `System.Reflection` namespace, and the other is the `Type` class itself. We're going to look at each of these options.

Before we carry on, you should be aware of the fact that you may stumble upon code in the following sections and throughout the chapter (and during your own development times) that invokes and modifies private members of an object. Quite a shock for those of you who've come a long way from a very strict object-oriented world programming background (C++ anyone?), where trespassing was not allowed. Accessing private fields, properties or methods directly was not allowed; manipulation of them via public accessor methods or properties was encouraged (because it provided a way to check that the user was modifying the data correctly).

Although .NET generally also encourages this style of object-oriented coding, in reflection it also gives developers the ability to "break the rules" in order to create powerful applications or overcome problems, like the one we talked about the start of the chapter.

Invoking Methods Using MethodInfo

We've come across the `MethodInfo` class before. What's so fascinating about this class is, that not only does it provide you with *all* metadata related to a single method, but it also provides you with the `Invoke()` method that can be used for all our dynamic method invocations. Needless to say, to be able to invoke a method using the `Invoke()` method, you'll need a valid `MethodInfo` instance pointing to an existing method or you'll see some nasty runtime errors you *don't* want to see.

The `MethodInfo.Invoke()` method has several overloaded forms, although the most common takes two arguments:

```
Invoke(obj As Object, parameters() As Object) As Object
```

The first parameter is the instance of the object that the method belongs to. However, if the method you want to invoke has an access type of Shared, you should ignore it by passing a null reference (Nothing in Visual Basic.NET) to it. The second parameter is a list of parameters to be passed to the invoking method. The parameters passed should be the same order and type as the parameters of the method being invoked. However, if the method takes no parameters, the second argument should be passed a null reference (Nothing) so that it's ignored. After the method is invoked, the returned value is of type Object that must be cast to the correct type before use. For instance, if you have a method called Multiply(), in a class called MathClass, which takes two Integers as parameters and returns an Integer after multiplying the two, you would invoke it the following way:

```
Dim objMathClass As New MathClass()
Dim params As Object() = {4, 5}
Dim method As MethodInfo = _
    objMathClass.GetType().GetMethod("Multiply")
Dim result As Integer

result = CInt(method.Invoke(objMathClass, params))
```

Note that the Multiply() method has to be declared Public for this to work, or your program will fail at runtime. This is because we didn't specify any binding flags, so GetMethod() used default bindings and searched for public members of the type only. And since GetMethod() returned a null reference, Invoke() will fail. To be able to set binding flags manually, you may use an overload of the GetMethod() method that accepts a combination of binding flags for searching for the correct method.

Consider the following code snippet for the same code shown above, with the assumption that this time, Multiply() as been declared with shared access:

```
Dim objMathClass As New MathClass()
Dim params As Object() = {4, 5}
Dim method As MethodInfo = GetType(MathClass).GetMethod("Multiply", _
                                    BindingFlags.NonPublic Or _
                                    BindingFlags.Static)
Dim result As Integer

result = CInt(method.Invoke(Nothing, params))
```

Notice how we explicitly requested GetMethod() to look for a Non-Public (Private) member which is also declared with a Static (shared) access type. We then invoked our method, passing a null reference as the first argument, as we're invoking a shared function and it doesn't require an instance of the type.

Using MethodInfo is one way of invoking methods dynamically. We'll see what other way there is as we move on through the chapter.

Invoking Properties Using PropertyInfo

Properties in a type can be defined as private, public, shared etc. They're one way of letting us "in" the object and allowing us to modify internal members of the type in a very safe, secure manner. Since this section is going to teach us *how* to invoke them using reflection (and we'll look at a real-world situation later in the chapter), let's look at the table below which shows how we may do so at runtime, using the PropertyInfo class.

There are two methods of the PropertyInfo class that are useful for manipulating property values:

❑ GetValue() – gets the value of the underlying property

❑ SetValue() – sets the underlying property to a new value

Below we show one of the two overloaded SetValue() methods with its signature:

```
SetValue(obj as Object, NewValue as Object, index() as Object)
```

You'll most likely find yourself modifying a property's value with the method shown. Similar to what we saw using the Invoke() method of MethodInfo, the first parameter of the SetValue() method accepts the instance whose property value is to be set. The second parameter takes the new value to be set for the property, and the third parameter takes an indexer for indexed properties. Non-indexed properties should have this third parameter set to a null reference (Nothing).

Likewise, the GetValue() method is used for retrieving a property's value. Its signature is shown below:

```
GetValue(obj as Object, index() as Object) as Object
```

The first parameter is the instance of the object we're trying to invoke, while the second parameter is an indexer representing indexed properties. Again, this should be set to Nothing if not applicable.

Let's have a look at a trivial example that uses the PropertyInfo class to invoke properties in a class. Below shows a simple class that implements a single private property, Name. We use an instance of this class in our Main() subroutine to get a valid PropertyInfo object and then use it to invoke the single private property it encapsulates:

```
Imports System
Imports System.Reflection

Public Class Human
    Private strName As String
```

```
    Private Property Name() As String
      Get
        Return strName
      End Get
      Set(ByVal Value As String)
            strName = Value
      End Set
    End Property
  End Class
```

Next, our main program begins by first instantiating the Human class and then grabbing hold of a valid PropertyInfo associated with the private property Name. Notice how we specifically tell the GetProperty() method of the Type class that the property we're searching for is an instance property (a property that can only be accessed through an instance of the type) and that its access type is non-public:

```
Public Class PropExample
  Public Shared Sub Main()
    Dim NewHuman As New Human()
    Dim prop As PropertyInfo

    prop = NewHuman.GetType.GetProperty("Name", _
                                BindingFlags.Instance Or _
                                BindingFlags.NonPublic)
```

We then declare a parameter of type String and initialize it with a value. Note that we could have used an Object type here as well since that would cast into the target type, which is a String in our case, correctly. But it is recommended that you use the same as that of the target type. The parameter is then passed to the SetValue() method for the property to be invoked and modified:

```
      Dim param As String = "Fahad"
      prop.SetValue(NewHuman, param, Nothing)
```

We finish by displaying the value of the Name property of our object by invoking the GetValue() method. The method returns an Object type that we explicitly cast into a String:

```
      Console.WriteLine(prop.GetValue(NewHuman, Nothing).ToString)
    End Sub
End Class
```

Invoking Fields Using FieldInfo

Like PropertyInfo, the FieldInfo class also contains GetValue() and SetValue() methods that we can use to manipulate field values. They have similar signatures to the PropertyInfo methods too, although there are no indexer-related parameters:

```
GetValue(obj As Object) as Object
SetValue(obj As Object, value as Object)
```

The `GetValue()` method takes a single argument, the instance of the type you're invoking.

> *Before we continue, a note about accessing private fields using reflection. We all know that the private fields of a class are not normally directly accessible outside the class, and are often only made accessible via properties or methods. However, say the recommended way of setting the value of the field (via an accessor method) involves a lot of extra fancy logic that you're not interested in or that might significantly slow your application down. The best way to sneak in would be using reflection; "breaking the rules" and accessing or modifying the field at will. Of course, you should be wary of doing this, as the available accessor method may contain input validation that we're bypassing by modifying the field directly. However, if you are building a debugging application that examines and loads different custom controls at runtime and allows you to modify and test their fields with a range of values, accessing and modifying them using reflection may be the most efficient option.*

Consider the code snippet below:

```
Dim objFoo As New Foo()
Dim field As FieldInfo = objFoo.GetType.GetField("PrivateField", _
                            . BindingFlags.NonPublic Or _
                            BindingFlags.Instance)
Console.WriteLine(field.GetValue(objFoo).ToString)
...
field.SetValue(objFoo, "New value")
```

We instantiate a type and get a private field by calling the `GetField()` method. We specify what field we're looking for, `PrivateField` in this case, and tell it that our field is a private instance member. We then call the `GetValue()` method of `FieldInfo` to get the value of the field and display it on the console. The last line of code sets our private field to a new value by passing it the instance of the object we're invoking and the new value.

Invoking Class Members Using InvokeMember()

The `Type` class exposes a powerful and flexible method in the Reflection API, namely the `InvokeMember()` method. This method allows you to invoke a reflected member of the supplied type (fields, properties, and methods). This is because all dynamic invocations you've seen so far using `MethodInfo`, `PropertyInfo` or `FieldInfo`, can all be performed using the `InvokeMember()` method. This is made possible by switching between the binding flags passed to the method during invocation.

If that's the case, you must be wondering why we bothered discussing the info classes for this purpose when we could have just relied on InvokeMember(). Well, that's where the down side of InvokeMember() comes in. You can definitely make all sorts of dynamic calls to any member of a type via InvokeMember(), but if you want to play around with and examine metadata and then invoke members dynamically it may be easier to use the info classes. However, since we're mainly concerned with dynamic invocation of members at the moment, let's find out more about this useful method and learn how to use it. In our next section we'll see how this can be implemented in a more real-word fashion.

The InvokeMember() method comes with a total of three overloads. Most likely, you'll find yourself using just one of its overloaded methods. This is shown below:

```
InvokeMember(name As String, invokeAttr As BindingFlags, _
        binder As Binder, target As Object, params() as Object)
```

This overload accepts five parameters. The first parameter describes the member to be invoked. This can be a property name, a method name or a field name. The second parameter is a single or a combination of different binding flags that tell the method how to search for the desired member and also tells the method what to treat the member as. For example, a BindingFlags.InvokeMethod flag would tell the method that the first parameter supplied is the name of the method to be invoked.

The third parameter accepts a Binder object. A Binder object can be explicitly created that can be used for binding to specific fields or methods from a list of overloads, and can also be used for specific type conversions of supplied arguments. If we pass Nothing (a null reference) to this parameter, the method automatically uses the DefaultBinder available. DefaultBinder takes care of type conversions of supplied arguments for us (conversions from source type to target types).

The fourth parameter takes the instance of the type whose member we're invoking. This should be supplied as Nothing if dealing with shared members of a type. The last parameter accepts an array of parameters to be passed to the invoked member. This can be used when dealing with properties or methods. When invoking fields, this parameter should be supplied as Nothing.

Invoking Methods Using InvokeMember()

Let's look at a code excerpt that uses the InvokeMember() method of the Type class to invoke a method of a type. The following code uses the type System.Math and invokes its shared method Max(). This method has eleven overloads and accepts different combinations of arguments. We'll see how our InvokeMember() method finds and matches the correct one depending on the type of arguments we pass it. For demonstration purposes, we're going to pass two integers to the method. Take a look:

```
Dim MathType As Type = GetType(System.Math)
Dim params As Object() = {5, 8}
Dim result As Integer

result = CInt(MathType.InvokeMember("Max", BindingFlags.Public Or _
                                   BindingFlags.InvokeMethod Or _
                                   BindingFlags.Static, Nothing, _
                                   Nothing, params))
Console.WriteLine(result)
```

As you can see, we invoked the method by explicitly adding the
`BindingFlags.InvokeMethod` flag to tell `InvokeMember` that the first parameter
passed is the name of a method we want to invoke. We passed `Nothing` as an object
instance which tells `InvokeMember()` that the given method has a shared access and
does not need an instance. The last parameter we passed was declared as an array of
`Objects`, holding values of two integers. You should be aware that unlike
`MethodInfo.Invoke()`, `InvokeMember()` has greater flexibility especially when it
comes to sending arguments over to the method to be invoked. This method takes care
of all implicit type conversions from the source type to the target type, and does an
implicit search on overloaded methods by matching the number and type of
parameters of the target method with the ones supplied. The returned result is cast to
an `Integer` and displayed on the console.

Notice how simple and subtle this was. All we have to take care about is that we
supply the correct binding flags during invocation. If the
`BindingFlags.InvokeMethod` flag was omitted or replaced with some other flag,
this wouldn't have worked.

The main advantage of using `InvokeMember()` is its flexibility. If we had tried using
similar code with a `MethodInfo` object, the code would have failed miserably giving us
an `AmbiguousMatchException` since it wouldn't be able to tell which overloaded
method to call. For that, we would have to explicitly declare a `Binder` object and use its
`SelectMethod()` method to search for an appropriate overloaded method and invoke
it. On the contrary, this was all taken care of by `InvokeMember()` method. It looked at
the number of arguments we supplied, examined the argument types, matched the
correct method from the list of overloads and – hey presto – invoked the method.

InvokeMember() Method Invocation Example

Near the start of the chapter, we discussed some very tempting features of dynamic
method invocation and suggested its use in a number of situations and scenarios. It's
about time we started looking at some and see how these features can accent our
applications to become more flexible, easy to extend and implement. We're going to
precede this section by modeling a real-world situation, where reflection could prove
to be more of a "solution" than just fancy talk.

We're going to use a variation on the user input-checking scenario we discussed at the start of the chapter. Briefly, we will have a "Scuba Diving" registration form to be filled in by applicants. The application involves a Windows Form that includes a number of different controls. Once the applicant decides to submit the information on the form to be filed and reviewed, we need to check if all the compulsory items on the form had been completed before the form was dismissed. Since we need to establish some code that accepts different controls at runtime to check and see if the control's not empty, reflection would be the best choice (amongst other alternatives we'll discuss later in the chapter) for deciding which method should be invoked for the type of control that's passed. Therefore we will code up a bunch of input-checking methods that take different control types as parameters, select the appropriate one using reflection at runtime, and invoke it.

There are several other advantages of this approach. You could later extend your code by introducing new or more controls and you'll have to make no changes to the 'control checking mechanism'. You could also think of compiling these methods into a separate assembly and invoke them with any application you develop. (We'll learn more about this in our next chapter).

To begin with, create a new Windows Application using Visual Studio.NET. Call it MethodInvocation and open the Design View of the form. Using the Toolbox, drag controls onto your form so that it looks similar to the one shown below:

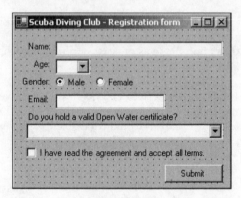

Following is the list of controls used by our application, along with their names:

Control Type	Name	Initial Text value
Label	Label1	"Name:"
Label	Label2	"Age:"
Label	Label3	"Gender:"
Label	Label4	"Email:"

Control Type	Name	Initial Text value
Label	Label5	"Do you hold a valid Open Water certificate?"
TextBox	txtName	Empty
ComboBox	comboAge	Filled with values ranging 15 to 60
RadioButton	radioButton1	"Male"
RadioButton	radioButton2	"Female"
TextBox	txtEmail	Empty
ComboBox	comboQuestion	Filled with three optional answers
Button	button1	"Submit"
CheckBox	checkAgreement	"I have read the agreement and accept all terms"

Once you're done adding controls onto your form, open up the form code and make sure you include the `System.Reflection` namespace into your project:

```
Imports System
Imports System.Reflection
```

Next, add a single field called `ErrorInForm` to the form class. We'll later make use of this variable to count the numbers of controls that have been left empty at the time the user submits the form:

```
Public Class Form1
    Inherits System.Windows.Forms.Form

    Private ErrorInForm As Integer = 0
```

Double-click on the form in order to create the `Form1_Load()` method. Since this method is called at the time the application loads, we're going to use it for initializing our controls, namely the two `ComboBox` controls: `comboAge` and `comboQuestion`. We make sure the controls are initialized with values so that our user may choose the correct one at the time of registration.

```
Private Sub Form1_Load(ByVal sender As System.Object, ByVal e As _
                       System.EventArgs) Handles MyBase.Load
    Dim i As Integer
    For i = 15 To 60
        comboAge.Items.Add(i)
    Next
```

```
      comboQuestion.Items.Add( _
                        "Yes, I currently hold a valid certificate")
      comboQuestion.Items.Add("No, I don't have one at the moment")
      comboQuestion.Items.Add( _
                        "I hold a temporary allowance certificate")
   End Sub
```

Here is the part where we implement our dynamic methods. Copy the following list of methods into your form class:

```
   'Handle all TextBoxes
   Private Sub ValidateField(ByVal control As TextBox)
      If control.Text.Trim.Equals("") Then
         ErrorInForm += 1
         control.BackColor = Color.Yellow()
      Else
         control.BackColor = Color.White()
      End If
   End Sub

   'Handle all ComboBoxes
   Private Sub ValidateField(ByVal control As ComboBox)
      If control.Text.Trim.Equals("") Then
         ErrorInForm += 1
         control.BackColor = Color.Yellow()
      Else
         control.BackColor = Color.White()
      End If
   End Sub

   'Handle all CheckBoxes
   Private Sub ValidateField(ByVal control As CheckBox)
      If Not control.Checked Then
         ErrorInForm += 1
      End If
   End Sub

   'Other unhandled controls
   Private Sub ValidateField(ByVal control As Label)
   End Sub

   Private Sub ValidateField(ByVal control As Button)
   End Sub

   Private Sub ValidateField(ByVal control As RadioButton)
   End Sub
End Class
```

As you can see, these methods all have the same base name: `ValidateField`. However, each one of these accepts different controls as parameters and then handles each control separately. For the one directly shown below, the method takes in a control of type `TextBox` and checks if its `Text` property is empty. If it is, we increment the error counter (`ErrorInForm` variable) and highlight the background color of the control. Similarly, in the case of a `ComboBox`, we check if its `Text` property is empty, and in the case of a `CheckBox` we make sure it's checked. The rest of the methods (for `Label`, `Button` and `RadioButton` controls) are left untouched as we're not interested in validating their controls. Note that we could add any number of methods to this list to handle other controls. For instance, a `ListBox` control would require different validation checks and so a method can be implemented to handle that separately too. As we'll see next, using these methods, we can use reflection to dynamically identify the type of the control and invoke the appropriate one, and the method that's invoked can handle the rest.

Next we have a set of handlers for different control types. All we need to do is invoke the correct one at runtime. We do this in the `button1_Click()` event. To implement this, simply switch to design mode again and double-click on the "Submit" button. This should place your cursor back in the code again, in the method `button1_Click`. Copy the highlighted text, compile your project and run it.

```
Private Sub button1_Click(ByVal sender As System.Object, _
    ByVal e As System.EventArgs) Handles button1.Click
  Try
    Dim FormControl As Control
    For Each FormControl In Me.Controls
      Me.GetType().InvokeMember("ValidateField", _
                      BindingFlags.Instance Or _
                      BindingFlags.InvokeMethod Or _
                      BindingFlags.NonPublic, Nothing, _
                      Me, New Object() {FormControl})
    Next

    If ErrorInForm = 0 Then
        MsgBox("Application has been processed. Thank you.", , _
            "Scuba Registration")
    Else
      MsgBox( _
            "There was at least one error in processing the form." & _
            " Please check again.", , "Scuba Registration")
      ErrorInForm = 0
    End If

  Catch ex As Exception
    'Catch exception here
  End Try
End Sub
```

In this method, we're performing a very simple task. For each of the child controls present on the form, we instruct the `InvokeMember()` method to invoke the correct `ValidateField()` method, depending on the type of control that was passed as an argument. Via reflection, `InvokeMember()` matches all available `ValidateField` methods for the correct type, selects the correct one and invokes it in a dynamic fashion.

The above code will produce the following output if we forget to fill in the Age and Email fields before clicking Submit.

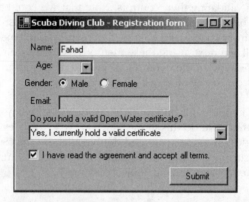

You can tell from the approach that reflection can most certainly help us overcome a lot of problems we'd face otherwise. On top of that, in scenarios where we're dealing with an external source, such as a database or an XML file, we can use this approach to handle incoming streams of data dynamically, and invoke correct handlers (or events) on the type of data we receive.

Manipulating Property Values Using InvokeMember()

`InvokeMember` goes beyond just dynamic method invocation. We can access and modify property values of an object by tweaking the binding flags we pass to it during invocation. Since there isn't much different between a call made to modify a property and a call made to invoke a method, let's hit some code straight away.

The code shown below invokes two properties of an object. The first one is a `Private Shared` property and we try to get its value by using the `Bindings.GetProperty` flag.

```
Dim FooType As Type = GetType(Foo)
Dim result As String

result = CStr(FooType.InvokeMember("PrivateShared", _
                        BindingFlags.NonPublic Or _
                        BindingFlags.Static Or _
                        BindingFlags.GetProperty, _
                        Nothing, Nothing, Nothing))
```

The second one, shown below, is a `Public Instance` property and we try to set a new value to it by using the `Bindings.SetProperty` flag:

```
Dim objFoo As New Foo()
Dim params As Object() = {"New Value"}
FooType.InvokeMember("PublicInstance", BindingFlags.Public Or _
                     BindingFlags.Instance Or _
                     BindingFlags.SetProperty, _
                     Nothing, objFoo, params)
```

The same rule applies to invoking properties via `InvokeMember()` as it did for invoking methods; that if there were a number of properties with the same base name but different signatures, `InvokeMember()` implicitly matches the correct property and invokes it.

It's worth mentioning here that properties in the .NET Framework are more or less regarded as methods. For instance, if you tried examining all public methods of an instance of a `TextBox` control, you'd be provided with all available public methods such as `Copy()`, `Cut()` along with methods that have a prefix of "get_" and "set_". These methods are actually public properties of the instance. For example, the `Text` property of the `TextBox` control would be shown as two methods: `get_Text()` and `set_Text()`. Since these properties are exposed as methods, we can invoke them using a `MethodInfo` object or by using the `InvokeMember()` of the `Type` class by supplying the `BindingFlags.InvokeMethod` flag. Have a look at the following line of code that displays the power of using `InvokeMember()`. It shows the `Text` property of an instance of a `TextBox` control being invoked and treated as a method:

```
TextBoxType.InvokeMember("get_Text", BindingFlags.Public Or _
                         BindingFlags.Instance Or _
                         BindingFlags.InvokeMethod, _
                         Nothing, txtBox1, Nothing)
```

InvokeMember() Property Value Modification Example

Many IDEs come with integrated property pages, that allow you to set initial values and configure object properties at design time. What's so interesting about these property pages is that they accommodate any type of object or component and expose their internal properties to be viewed and modified. For example, while developing Windows Applications, you probably fill your form with a number of controls. Each time you click on a different control, the property viewer refreshes its contents and exposes all available properties of that object type. Behind the scenes, this nifty little tool is actually using reflection to reflect all properties and every time a property is modified, it invokes the property of that particular instance and passes the new argument to it.

To get the idea across, we're going to make our very own Property Page that will reflect the loaded type's properties and allow us to modify them. However, since this book is really not about making controls and making a full-fledged property page would cross chapter boundaries, we're going to implement a very basic type of property page using a `TreeView`, a `TextBox` and a `Button` control.

For our example, we're going to implement a test class that we'll use with our Property Page, but you can later use the idea to extend the application and use it for loading types at runtime.

Create a new Windows Application, and call it `ReflectProperties`. Create a form that looks similar to the one shown below:

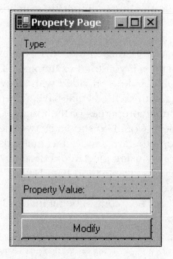

Following is the list of controls used by this application, along with their names and values:

Control Type	Name	Initial Text value
Label	Label1	"Property Value:"
Label	Label2	"Type:"
TreeView	TreeView1	Empty
TextBox	TextBox1	Empty
Button	Button1	"Modify"

Add the `System.Reflection` namespace to your form code:

```
Imports System
Imports System.Reflection
```

Before we look at our code in the main public class, we create a small test class for our purpose. We'll instantiate and use this class for demonstrating property invocation in objects.

```
Public Class Test

    ' Set Default private values
    Private MyName As String = "Fahad"
    Private MyAge As String = "22"
    Private MyCountry As String = "Pakistan"

    Public Property Name() As String
      Get
         Return Me.MyName
      End Get
      Set(ByVal Value As String)
         Me.MyName = Value
      End Set
    End Property

    Public Property Age() As String
      Get
         Return Me.MyAge
      End Get
      Set(ByVal Value As String)
         Me.MyAge = Value
      End Set
    End Property

    Public Property Country() As String
      Get
         Return Me.MyCountry
      End Get
      Set(ByVal Value As String)
         Me.MyCountry = Value
      End Set
    End Property
End Class
```

The Test class has three public properties and three private variables corresponding to them. The private variables, all String variables, have been initialized with default values. Now we move onto implementing the main public class.

To use the instance of the Test class, we declare a Shared object as a class variable, MyObj, shown below. Also, we add a string to our class, SelectedNode, with class scope. This is because every time the user selects a new property, the TreeView1_AfterSelect event will be launched and we need to make sure we save the name of the current property selected so that we may use this information while we invoke the property:

```
Public Class Form1
    Inherits System.Windows.Forms.Form

    Public Shared MyObj As Object
    Private SelectedNode As String
```

Next, to be able to use our sample class we need to instantiate it in the `Form1_Load()` event, since that's the first method called when the form is loaded. The `Form1_Load()` method is used for instantiating our shared object – `MyObj` – that we earlier declared as a class variable, and it can be added to the form class by double clicking on the form.

```
Private Sub Form1_Load(ByVal sender As System.Object, ByVal e As _
                    System.EventArgs) Handles MyBase.Load
    MyObj = New Test()

    ReflectProperties(MyObj.GetType)
End Sub
```

Notice that we also make a call to the `ReflectProperties()` method in `Form1_Load()`. This method is shown below. Note that `ReflectProperties()` is passed the type of the object we're using, which it uses for reflecting all public properties of the type onto our `TreeView` control.

```
Private Sub ReflectProperties(ByVal MyType As Type)
    Dim properties As PropertyInfo() = MyType.GetProperties()
    Dim prop As PropertyInfo

    TreeView1.BeginUpdate()

    ' Fill tree with property names
    For Each prop In properties
        TreeView1.Nodes.Add(New TreeNode(prop.Name))
    Next

    TreeView1.EndUpdate()

End Sub
```

Every time the user selects a node on the `TreeView` control, the `TreeView1_AfterSelect()` event is launched. We need to make sure every time this happens, we get the chosen node (corresponding to a property) and reflect its value in the `TextBox` control. In this method, we save the name of the node in the string class variable we declared earlier, and use the `GetProperty()` method of the `Type` class to return a `PropertyInfo` object for the underlying property. Near the end of the method, we use the `GetValue()` method of `PropertyInfo` to display the returned value of the property in the `Textbox` control on the form.

```
' Show value of property when property is selected
Private Sub TreeView1_AfterSelect(ByVal sender As System.Object, _
    ByVal e As System.Windows.Forms.TreeViewEventArgs) _
    Handles TreeView1.AfterSelect

    SelectedNode = e.Node.Text

    Dim PropInfo As PropertyInfo = _
        MyObj.GetType.GetProperty(SelectedNode)

    TextBox1.Text = PropInfo.GetValue(MyObj, Nothing)
End Sub
```

The code below deals with the modification part of the Property Page. We'll be implementing this in the Click event handler of the Modify button, which we can generate automatically in VS.NET by double clicking on the button.

Here, we simply call the InvokeMember() method of Type and pass BindingFlags.SetProperty as one of the binding flags. Note that the new value to be set to the property is taken from the Textbox control on our form and is passed as a variable of type Object.

```
Private Sub Button1_Click(ByVal sender As System.Object, ByVal e As _
                          System.EventArgs) Handles Button1.Click

    ' Get new value from TextBox
    Dim NewValue As Object() = {TextBox1.Text}

    ' Set new value to the property
    MyObj.GetType.InvokeMember(SelectedNode, _
                      BindingFlags.SetProperty Or _
                      BindingFlags.Instance Or _
                      BindingFlags.Public, _
                      Nothing, MyObj, NewValue, Nothing)

    TreeView1.Refresh()
End Sub
```

If you run the application you will see the following:

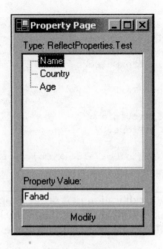

You should be able to click on any properties in the tree to view a property value, and you can modify it by writing the new value in the text box and clicking the Modify button.

Manipulating Field Values Using InvokeMember()

We shall once again look at a trivial code snippet that shows InvokeMember() invoking fields in a loaded type. To do this, we will once again concentrate only on the binding flags and make sure we include the BindingFlags.GetField flag to our list of flags to retrieve the value of the specified field, or BindingFlags.SetField to set the value of the specified field. The code for setting a value of a private, shared field is shown below:

```
Dim FooType As Type = GetType(Foo)
Dim params As Object() = {"New Value"}

FooType.InvokeMember("PublicInstance", BindingFlags.NonPublic Or _
                                       BindingFlags.Static Or _
                                       BindingFlags.SetField, _
                                       Nothing, Nothing, params)
```

It is clear that the InvokeMember() method of the Type class is undoubtedly superior to other available invocation methods when it comes to pure dynamic invocation. It is highly flexible, powerful and does the job in a simple manner. You should try using this method over other invocation methods (exposed by the info classes) as much as possible, unless of course you need to be dealing with the metadata, in which case you'll be bound to use other available classes such as MethodInfo, PropertyInfo or FieldInfo.

InvokeMember() Field Value Modification Example

In this section, we're going to build a runnable example that shows how fields can be directly invoked in certain cases. The application that we're going to look at models a terminal program at a car retailer. There are a number of forms with different questions the customer has to answer before he may place an order for a car. However, we're going to be concerned with, supposedly, only the final form of the questionnaire where the customer is asked to select a car model along with a number of optional features (these will be referred to as fields in our implementation) that come along with it. For example, let's say the customer selects the 1999 model. That model had two optional features (fields): the car could be a convertible and could have a built-in refrigerator. The customer can select either one, or both of them, and choose to submit his application to be lodged. The selection the customer makes will be saved via reflection by dynamically modifying the fields.

What's so dynamic about the application we're about to see is that our main program will have no clue to what type of model our user will decide to select at runtime. In fact, it is at runtime that our program will load a list of available car models (defined by different classes), and upon the user's selection, it will dynamically select the correct class, search for all available fields (optional features for that model) at runtime, and then populate a `CheckedListBox` with all available fields found. Similarly, upon modification made by the user to any field, the modification will be saved via dynamic invocation and the form will be processed.

The advantage of this approach is that this system is completely independent of the car models available, since it loads all available models at runtime and invokes the appropriate one using reflection, and so the system can be extended by all means. New car models can be introduced to the list without making any changes to your code.

Let's now look at the code and see how it's done.

Create a new Windows Application and name your project `InvokingFields`. Add controls to your form so that it looks like the form shown below:

Following is the list of controls used by this application, along with their names and values:

Control Type	Name	Initial Text value
Label	Label1	"Select a Model:"
Label	Label2	"Please Select Optional Specifications:"
ComboBox	ComboxBox1	Empty
CheckedListBox	CheckedListBox1	Empty
Button	Button1	"Modify Options & Buy Car"

Start off by adding the `System.Reflection` namespace to your form code:

```
Imports System
Imports System.Reflection
```

Next add the following `Cars` class that contains a list of nested classes that represent car models. Each class holds definitions of some `Shared` fields (optional features of the model). Note that fields can be added or subtracted from the classes without changing the code that invokes these classes.

```
Public Class Cars

  'Previous models come here

  Public Class Model_1999
     'Optional or Customizable items
     Public Shared Refrigerator As Boolean
     Public Shared Convertible As Boolean = True

  End Class

  Public Class Model_2000
     'Optional or Customizable items
     Public Shared Automatic_Windows As Boolean

  End Class

  Public Class Model_2001
     'Optional or Customizable items
     Public Shared Dvd_Player As Boolean
  End Class

  End Class
```

Invoking Members Dynamically

The reason why I chose to nest these classes in the main `Cars` class is for demonstration purposes. We will see how we can use reflection to get a list of nested classes from within a parent class in the `Form1_Load()` method below. Also, since the code was intended to be dynamic and choosing an external source to load a list of car models didn't seem like a very good idea, this approach should allow you to think in broader terms and show you how powerful reflection can be.

Now, entering the form class, add the following line to declare a field, `SelectedType` of type `Type`. This variable will hold the type of the car model the user selects at runtime:

```
Public Class Form1
     Inherits System.Windows.Forms.Form

     Public SelectedType As Type
```

Next, create the `Form1_Load()` method by double clicking the form. In this method we perform the basic tasks of loading available car model types and filling the `ComboBox` control with them. Here we introduce you to a new method of the `Type` class, the `GetNestedTypes()` method. This method accepts a combination of binding flags, searches for types nested within the supplied type and returns an array of types found (this is empty if no types are found). We can also use the `GetNestedType()` method to search for a single type. In the code below, we retrieve all nested types inside `Cars` and display their names in the `ComboBox` control. Initially, the `Button` control is disabled (we don't want the user clicking it right away without selecting a model – in other words, we haven't implemented any checks!).

```
Private Sub Form1_Load(ByVal sender As System.Object, _
    ByVal e As System.EventArgs) Handles MyBase.Load

Dim MyType As Type = GetType(Cars)

'Get the Nested classes with the Access-Specifier as public.
Dim NestedClasses As Type() = _
    MyType.GetNestedTypes(BindingFlags.Public Or _
                          BindingFlags.Instance)
Dim NestedClass As Type

For Each NestedClass In NestedClasses
   ComboBox1.Items.Add(NestedClass.Name)
Next

Button1.Enabled = False
End Sub
```

Every time the user selects a different car model from the dropdown combo box; the `ComboBox1_SelectedIndexChanged` event will be launched, and every time he'll be shown the fields (features) associated with that type. For that reason, we'll perform all our basic "reflect fields" routines in the `ComboBox1_SelectedIndexChanged()` method:

```
Private Sub ComboBox1_SelectedIndexChanged( _
    ByVal sender As System.Object, ByVal e As System.EventArgs) _
    Handles ComboBox1.SelectedIndexChanged

  Dim SelectedModel As String = _
      "InvokingFields.Cars+" & ComboBox1.SelectedItem

  SelectedType = Type.GetType(SelectedModel)

  Dim fields As FieldInfo() = SelectedType.GetFields()
  Dim i As Integer

  CheckedListBox1.Items.Clear()
  For i = 0 To fields.Length - 1
    CheckedListBox1.Items.Add(fields(i).Name)
    If fields(i).GetValue(Nothing) = True Then
      CheckedListBox1.SetItemChecked(i, True)
    End If
  Next

  Button1.Enabled = True
End Sub
```

The important work is being done inside the For loop here. We obtain an array of FieldInfo objects from the GetFields() method and, for each field discovered, it is added to the CheckedListBox control's items list. At the same time we perform a single check to see if the current field's value is True. If it is, we check the corresponding field name in the CheckedListBox control.

For the rest of the method, you're probably familiar with most of the code, except for the following lines of code:

```
Dim SelectedModel As String = _
    "InvokingFields.Cars+" & ComboBox1.SelectedItem
SelectedType = Type.GetType(SelectedModel)
```

What we're doing here is actually very straightforward. The SelectedItem property of the ComboxBox returns the item that the user selected from the dropdown. For instance, if the user selected Model_1999 from the dropdown, that's just what ComboBox1.SelectedItem will return. However, we have to obtain a valid Type of the selected item so that we may invoke its fields. To do that, we use the Type.GetType() method which accepts a string describing the complete path of the class we're trying to discover. In our case, InvokingFields is the namespace and Cars is the class that contains other nested classes, so the access path to Cars from our namespace would be InvokingFields.Cars. The "+" sign, however, is used for accessing nested classes from within a parent class. Therefore, the complete path supplied to the Type.GetType() method turns out to be of the format:

```
InvokingFields.Cars+Model_XXXX
```

where XXXX is the model number.

Once the fields have been retrieved and reflected, the user can pick whichever feature he'd like for the model of the car he's buying. Upon clicking the Modify button, we go through a series of statements in the Button1_Click() event handler to make sure all modifications made are reflected back to the fields. In our code, we run through a loop for all items present in the CheckedListBox control and retrieve each item one by one. Each item in the list represents a single field, and so we use its name and its current value to invoke the corresponding field using the InvokeMember() method. Notice how we use the BindingFlags.SetField flag to tell InvokeMember() that we're interested in setting a new value for a field which has a Public and Shared access in the underlying type:

```
Private Sub Button1_Click(ByVal sender As System.Object, _
    ByVal e As System.EventArgs) Handles Button1.Click

  Dim i As Integer
  Dim FieldName As String
  Dim Field As FieldInfo

  For i = 0 To CheckedListBox1.Items.Count() - 1
    FieldName = CheckedListBox1.Items.Item(i)
    Dim Value As Object() = {CheckedListBox1.GetItemChecked(i)}

    SelectedType.InvokeMember(FieldName, BindingFlags.Public Or _
                              BindingFlags.Static Or _
                              BindingFlags.SetField, _
                              Nothing, Nothing, Value)
  Next
  MsgBox("Thank you. Your car order has been processed.")
End Sub
```

Once the button is clicked, the application ends with an approval message.

When you run the application and select a model, you should see something like this:

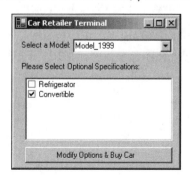

You will notice that the number of options, and the options themselves, change depending upon the model you select. If you then select your options and click the button, you will see an acknowledgement message.

In spite of our strong inclination towards using reflection in almost "all" messy situations, we're now going to switch places and look at reflection from a far end; let's see how reflection can sometimes *not* be the best option you have.

Reflective Invocation at a Price

Over the course of the chapter, we've seen reflection do some useful things, including dynamically searching and invoking members at runtime. However, there are some fairly "clumsy" aspects about reflection that sometimes are not very inviting when we look more closely at it. Talking about dynamic invocation of methods specifically, at times you may find (the hard way) that all the pain of writing lengthier code and spending hours trying to implement the "perfect" reflective solution didn't quite pay off in the end, especially when you discover several reasons why this might happen:

❑   Dynamic invocation features of reflection are not type-safe

❑   Sometimes, in some situations, there are better alternatives to using reflection (we'll talk about this shortly)

When we say reflection is not type-safe, we simply mean that the compiler will let you get away with most of the things (trying to access methods that don't exist, trying to modify a field with an invalid cast, and so on) it will usually complain about at compile-time, so what initially should have been a compile-time error will become a runtime error instead. However, in many ways that's just something we have to live with: the whole point about dynamic binding is that the type isn't known until runtime, so we can't check types at compile-time. You can't, as they say, have your cake *and* eat it.

Other than that, if you're creating a small-scale application, using reflection can be overkill – and adding unnecessary complexity to your code in this way may result in code that has more bugs, is slower, more difficult to maintain and less extensible.

Indeed, .NET offers you a type-safe alternative to reflective method invocation: using **delegates**. Our next section will discuss how delegates can be used for creating type-safe abstractions.

Reflection Or Delegates?

If you aren't that familiar with delegates, in short they're completely type-safe, secure managed objects that are used for invoking methods of other objects in a late binding fashion (sound familiar?). Sure, we can do this using `MethodInfo.Invoke()` or `Type.InvokeMember()` but one thing's for sure, we can't be absolutely sure our call will point to a valid method at runtime, and we won't find out until it gives us a runtime error – completely non type-safe and risky. On the other hand, we have delegates providing us with the same functionality and results (considerably faster too in most cases).

A delegate does just what its literal meaning suggests; it hands control over to the appropriate method when called. At the point of instantiating a delegate, it is passed a reference to the object to use and address of the method (of the loaded object) that is called indirectly when a call is made to the delegate. At the time of declaration, the compiler does a lot of background-work for you and creates a class for the delegate you declare. Every delegate exposes the `Invoke()` method, similar to what we saw using reflection, which is used for passing parameters to the correct method (static or instance method). However, what's so interesting about a delegate is that it does not treat static methods differently than it would treat instance methods. In contrast with reflection, if you remember, we had to tweak the binding flags around a bit to tell the method what type of call it is.

To see how using a delegate to invoke a method programmatically differs from using reflection, consider the following console application. This example shows the workings of a delegate, trying to dynamically invoke the correct method at runtime.

```
Imports System

' Declare a delegate
Public Delegate Function Invoker(ByVal x As Integer, _
    ByVal y As Integer) As Integer

Module Module1

    ' A Test class
    Private Class MyMath

        ' A shared method
        Public Shared Function Pow(ByVal x As Integer, _
                            ByVal y As Integer) As Integer
            Return x ^ y
        End Function

        ' An instance method
        Public Function Multiply(ByVal x As Integer, _
                            ByVal y As Integer) As Integer
            Return x * y
        End Function
```

```
    End Class

    Sub Main()
      Try
         Dim result As Object
         Dim x As Integer = 2
         Dim y As Integer = 3
         Dim objMath As New MyMath()

         ' Call instance method "Multiply"
         Dim MyDelegate As New Invoker(AddressOf objMath.Multiply)
         result = MyDelegate.Invoke(2, 3)
         Console.WriteLine("The product of {0} and {1} is: {2}", _
                            x, y, result)

         ' Call shared method "Pow"
         Dim MyDelegate2 As New Invoker(AddressOf MyMath.Pow)
         result = MyDelegate2.Invoke(x, y) ' Same as MyMath.Pow(args)
         Console.WriteLine("{0} to the power of {1} is: {2}", _
                            x, y, result)
      Catch e As Exception
         MsgBox(e.Message, , "Exception Caught")
      End Try
      Console.ReadLine()
    End Sub
End Module
```

The example produces the following output.

```
The product of 2 and 3 is: 6
2 to the power of 3 is: 8
```

As you can see, using a delegate to invoke methods is extremely simple. All we had to do was create an instance of our publicly defined delegate, as shown below, and pass it the address of the function to be called:

```
Public Delegate Function Invoker(ByVal x As Integer, _
                                 ByVal y As Integer) As Integer
```

The rest is taken care of by the runtime. Note that if you had passed an incorrect address of a method that did not exist, it would have given you a compile-time error rather than giving you a runtime error as it would have when using reflection. Also note that we didn't have to set any binding flags, worry about the wrong method being called or anything else. In fact, you can see how a delegate doesn't even distinguish between calls made to static or instance methods. See below:

```
Dim MyDelegate As New Invoker(AddressOf objMath.Multiply)
```

This is the same as the one below, with the only difference being the method invoked:

```
Dim MyDelegate2 As New Invoker(AddressOf MyMath.Pow)
```

It's interesting to consider how we might attempt to mimic the Invoke() method of the delegate class using reflection. Using reflection, we must indirectly invoke the correct method depending on the number and type of parameters passed. The Invoker class, implemented below, has equivalent functionality to a delegate class but uses reflection instead:

```
Imports System
Imports System.Reflection

Public Class Invoker

    ' Private variables to store received arguments from the constructor
    Private myType As Type
    Private myObject As Object
    Private myMethod As String

    ' In case of a static method invocation
    ' Constructor takes a type and a method name
    Public Sub New(ByVal TargetType As Type, _
                   ByVal TargetMethod As String)
      myType = TargetType
      myMethod = TargetMethod
    End Sub

    ' In case of an instance method invocation
    ' Constructor takes an object and a method name
    Public Sub New(ByVal TargetObject As Object, _
                ByVal TargetMethod As String)
      myObject = TargetObject
      myType = TargetObject.GetType()
      myMethod = TargetMethod
    End Sub

    ' Mimicking the Invoke method of a delegate
    Public Function Invoke(ByVal args As Object()) As Object

      If Not myType Is Nothing AndAlso Not myMethod = Nothing Then
        Dim myBindingFlags As Long
        myBindingFlags = _
            BindingFlags.InvokeMethod Or BindingFlags.Public

        If myObject Is Nothing Then
          myBindingFlags = myBindingFlags Or BindingFlags.Static
        Else
          myBindingFlags = myBindingFlags Or BindingFlags.Instance
        End If
        ' invoking the appropriate method
```

```vb
            Return myType.InvokeMember(myMethod, myBindingFlags, Nothing, _
                                 myObject, args)
       Else
          Throw New Exception("Incorrect parameter passed")
       End If

   End Function

End Class

Module Module1

   ' A Test class
   Private Class MyMath

      'A shared method
      Public Shared Function Pow(ByVal x As Integer, _
                                 ByVal y As Integer) As Integer
         Return x ^ y
      End Function

      'An instance method
      Public Function Multiply(ByVal x As Integer, _
                               ByVal y As Integer) As Integer
         Return x * y
      End Function

   End Class

   Sub Main()
      Try
         Dim result As Object
         Dim args As Object() = {2, 3}
         Dim objMath As New MyMath()

         Dim MyDelegate As New Invoker(objMath, "Multiply")
         result = MyDelegate.Invoke(args)
         Console.WriteLine("The product of {0} and {1} is: {2}", _
                        args(0), args(1), result)

         ' Call shared method "Pow"
         Dim objDelegate1 As New Invoker(GetType(MyMath), "Pow")
         result = objDelegate1.Invoke(args) ' Same as MyMath.Pow(args)
         Console.WriteLine("{0} to the power of {1} is: {2}", _
                        args(0), args(1), result)
      Catch e As Exception
         MsgBox(e.Message, , "Exception Caught")
      End Try
      Console.ReadLine()
   End Sub

End Module
```

As you can see, if delegates weren't there, this is how we'd implement one of our own. The `Invoker` class acts more or less like a delegate, using `Invoke()` to call the appropriate method after programmatically setting `BindingFlags` to decide which method to call. You've certainly seen how to dynamically invoke methods using reflection, but what's of more interest is the way we invoked it. Have a look at the code from the main subroutine below:

```
Dim MyDelegate As New Invoker(objMath, "Multiply")
result = MyDelegate.Invoke(args)
```

We instantiated a new `Invoker` object and passed its constructor a reference to the object to use along with a method name. We then called the `Invoke()` method of our "delegate" and passed a number of arguments. This call indirectly invoked the `Multiply()` method of the `Math` object we created. The call made to the `Invoke()` method is similar to the code below:

```
result = objMath.Multiply(args)
```

Or reflectively and more accurately:

```
result = myType.InvokeMember(Multiply, myBindingFlags, _
                             Nothing, objMath, args)
```

However, since our copy (`Invoker`) of the real delegate is still not type-safe and was much harder to implement, considering the size and scope of the problem at hand, we can see the advantages of using delegates.

It is important to note here that in spite of delegates having an advantage over reflection, they still are limited in their use. For example, a single delegate can cast only a single method signature at one time, meaning that if the method `Pow()` in our example took both parameters as `Double` rather than `Integer`, we would have been forced to declare another delegate specifically for that method. However, we do have the option of using **multicast** delegates. In this case you define a list of methods to be invoked by the delegate and they're all invoked at a single go, one by one. However, sometimes you really don't want that. Delegates also cannot be used as flexibly as we used reflection for modifying private members of an object.

As a conclusion, there really isn't a hard and fast rule for which technique to use when. For that you'll have to judge your application, and perceive if you'll ever need something as powerful as reflection to add ultimate "extendibility" to your applications. However, in general, it is recommended that for situations such as the one we just saw, you should avoid reflection and consider alternatives such as delegates.

Summary

In this chapter we discussed how to use reflection in an active way to control class members. We dived into the following topics:

- Reasons why we should consider using dynamic invocation techniques on types and their members

- How to dynamically invoke methods, properties and fields using `Type.InvokeMember()`

- How to dynamically invoke methods using `MethodInfo.Invoke()`

- How to dynamically modify fields and properties using the `GetValue()` and `SetValue()` methods of the `FieldInfo` and `PropertyInfo` classes

- Why using dynamic invocation via reflection is not always the best choice, and when we should use delegates instead

In the next chapter we are going to consider how to create objects using reflection.

VB.NET

Reflection

Handbook

4

4

Creating Objects

A powerful tool .NET presents to developers is dynamic assembly loading, which allows new code to be added to an application after compile time so that a new assembly can be plugged into an application on the fly. As with other dynamic programming techniques, there are pitfalls that can trap a programmer. But, with a thorough understanding of the technology, dynamic programming can lead to incredibly flexible and supportable applications.

This chapter describes first how to dynamically load an assembly in .NET. It covers some of the method calls that dynamically load the assemblies, as well as dynamic object creation, and then briefly describes how .NET loads class definitions under the hood. The next section discusses the abstract factory pattern, which is a very useful programming technique that helps us take advantage of dynamically loaded objects and helps create extremely flexible applications. The final section discusses how the combination of dynamically loaded objects and the abstract factory patterns can be used to design extremely flexible and manageable architectures, including a potential business need for a flexible application, and how it can be implemented in .NET.

Dynamic Assembly Loading

It is very common for applications to require a minor extension of functionality to be added after the release of an application. Usually this entails rewriting some segments of code to accommodate the changes, but significant retesting must be done to ensure that the previous functionality is intact. Consider an example of a web site that caters specifically to handheld devices with wireless connectivity. Unlike desktop browsers, the specifications for the HTML supported by such browsers is changing rapidly, since there are more platforms to support and capabilities are rapidly evolving as the devices become more powerful. A web site that caters to these users needs to be able to add support for the latest browsers, without affecting the other users. The ability to add a component that dynamically loads the software for each browser type could allow a web site to greatly reduce the amount of retesting that needs to be done when a new browser type is added.

The reflection library allows the programmer to dynamically load assemblies, by specifying an assembly name and version information. Since the .NET Framework checks the version of the assembly loaded, the old problems associated with "DLL Hell" (the source of many COM woes, where the incorrect version of a DLL is loaded by an application) are virtually eliminated. Binding an assembly to another assembly can happen either statically at design time, or dynamically at runtime. The static references are stored in the assembly's metadata when the assembly is built, while the dynamic references are created on the fly using a method such as `System.Reflection.Assembly.Load()`, as we will see later.

Creating Assembly References

Assemblies may be loaded either by fully referencing the assembly name, version, cultural environment, and public key token, or by partially referencing the assembly by omitting any of the attributes, except the name, which is required. Fully referencing an assembly is the best way to create a reference, since this guarantees the caller that the expected assembly will be loaded, eliminating potential "DLL Hell" situations. Statically referenced assemblies are always fully referenced – the compiler includes all of the assembly reference information in the referencing assembly's metadata.

Regardless of how an assembly reference is specified (dynamically or statically, fully or partially), the next step is for .NET to turn the assembly reference information into the location of a particular .NET assembly file – usually a DLL. So how does .NET find the DLL from the provided reference information?

Application Configuration Files and Binding

First, the runtime examines the application configuration files to see if they specify a DLL containing a particular named assembly. They can also help resolve full names from partial references, and give information about which version should be used. Assembly binding behavior can be configured at three levels based on these files:

❏ **Application Configuration File** – The standard .NET application configuration file.

❏ **Publisher Policy File** – These files can indicate a new assembly should be loaded in place of an old one. Useful to redirect previous assemblies to the latest version.

❏ **Machine Configuration File** – Settings that apply to the entire computer.

The second step is to check whether the assembly has been bound to beforehand, if so, the previously loaded version is used. Since the assembly name and other attributes match, you are guaranteed that this is the identical version that you are looking for, so there is no reason to reload the assembly. The Global Assembly Cache (GAC) is searched next, and if the assembly is found there, the runtime uses that assembly. If the assembly is not found in the GAC, the runtime **probes** for the assembly. Probing consists of searching the application path for a DLL containing the required assembly. The framework searches for a folder under the application root named the same as the assembly to be loaded. It also uses the culture to determine if the assembly's DLL is located in a folder with the same name as the culture.

The paths searched are as follows:

❏ [application base] / [assembly name] / [assembly name].dll

❏ [application base] / [culture] / [assembly name].dll

❏ [application base] / [culture] / [assembly name] / [assembly name].dll

Defining an AssemblyName

In order to load a fully referenced assembly dynamically, you need to create an AssemblyName object to specify which assembly to load. There are four main parameters that identify an assembly:

❏ Name

❏ Version

❏ Culture

❏ Strong Name or signature

```
' Create and populate the AssemblyName object
Dim assemblyName As New System.Reflection.AssemblyName()
assemblyName.Name = "TestAssembly"
```

You may specify a partial query without the version, culture, or strong name, however you are not guaranteed that the assembly will be unique, and the first assembly found matching those parameters will be returned. It is best practice to include every parameter to guarantee the assembly loaded is the one you intend to load.

93

The version parameter is an object of type Version that contains the major and minor version numbers, an optional build number, and an optional revision number. If the runtime finds an assembly with a higher build number, but the Major and Minor versions match, it will load that assembly.

❑   Major – Assemblies with the same name but different major versions are not interchangeable, so backward compatibility cannot be assumed.

❑   Minor – The new version offers a significant enhancement, but backward compatibility is maintained.

❑   Build – The number of the build of the same set of source code. Code could be rebuilt to optimize for a new processor, OS, or compiler feature. The code is compatible and the feature set should remain the same. If the code is a work in progress, the major and minor versions will remain the same, and the build number will be incremented for each build.

❑   Revision – A revision is meant to be interchangeable with the previous version, except with a possible hot patch for a bug or security hole, so the runtime will load an assembly with a higher revision number (but not a lower one).

```
assemblyName.Version = New Version("1.0.3300.0")
```

The Culture parameter specifies a CultureInfo class that determines the cultural environment that this code is intended to be run in. For example, the culture string en indicates English. We can provide different versions of an assembly designed to be used in different cultures, perhaps to provide different language support. A word processor might load its grammar checking, hyphenation, and spelling modules from an assembly, using the culture to specify the language required.

```
assemblyName.CultureInfo = New System.Globalization.CultureInfo("en")
```

The StrongName is a cryptographically sound signature of the compiled contents of an assembly. Strong naming relies on public key cryptography.

In public key cryptography, a public-private key pair is created. The public key can be used to decrypt data encrypted with the private key, and the private key can be used to decrypt data encrypted with the public key. The public key is given to everybody who might need to communicate with the person who owns the key, and the private key is kept secret by the owner. To digitally sign some data, the owner of the key takes a hash of the data, using a cryptographic hashing algorithm such as SHA or MD5. They then encrypt the hash (sometimes called a digest) using their private key, creating a digital signature. They can then distribute the original data, accompanied by the signature. Someone in possession of the public key, having received the data, can verify that it is the data that was originally signed by performing the same hashing process on the data, generating the same hash that the owner of the key created. They then decrypt the signature using the owner's public key, and if the result is the same as the hash, the signature is valid and the data is the same as the data the originator signed.

A strong name, then, is a digital signature derived from the entire compiled contents of the assembly. Because it is signed using a particular developer's private key, the strong name generated for a particular assembly can't be duplicated by anybody else, meaning you can't pass off a different assembly under the same strong name (even if you have the original developer's private key!).

Partially Referencing Assemblies

If some of the reference information is unavailable, an assembly can be loaded with only partial reference information. The simple name of the assembly is required, but the assembly can be loaded without the version, culture, or signature. Using a partial reference can be helpful in situations where you simple want to grab the latest version of the assembly, since the assembly with the highest version number will be loaded if the version is omitted. But it must be used carefully, since you are not guaranteed that the version of the assembly you are calling is compatible with the client. Creating a partial reference without the version information is not recommended, since it will load assemblies with major revision changes, which do not guarantee backward compatibility.

If the runtime loads an assembly with partial reference information, it will first search the application configuration file. The application configuration file may include the full reference. If so, the runtime proceeds with the full reference from the application configuration. This method can be useful in defining the version of the assembly to use without recompiling the assembly, but should not be used on assemblies that are shared among several applications. Since the runtime searches the configuration file at the application level and not the assembly level, every application configuration file needs the full updated assembly reference.

If the configuration file does not include the full reference, the runtime will search the application directory and then the GAC. If the version is not specified in the reference, the runtime will attempt to load the version with the highest version that matches the other criteria.

Methods Used For Dynamic Assembly Loading

In order to dynamically load an assembly into an application, one of the following methods must be used:

- ❑ `System.Reflection.Assembly.Load()`
- ❑ `System.Reflection.Assembly.LoadFrom()`
- ❑ `System.Reflection.Assembly.LoadWithPartialName()`

The `System.Reflection.Assembly.Load()` function can be used to either load a fully referenced assembly or partially referenced assembly. It takes a single `AssemblyName` object as a parameter, which the runtime uses to determine which assembly to load. The `LoadWithPartialName()` method differs from the `Load()` method in that it takes a string argument and skips the application configuration file lookup. The `LoadFrom()` method takes in a string argument that determines the path for the DLL file that holds the assembly.

```
' Load the assembly from the reflection library
oAssembly = System.Reflection.Assembly.Load(oAssemblyName)
```

```
' Load the assembly from the reflection library
' with a partial reference
partial = "TestAssembly,version=1.0.0.1001"
oAssembly = System.Reflection.Assembly.LoadWithPartialName(partial)
```

Instantiating Classes Dynamically

Once the assembly is loaded, you can create an instance of a class inside the assembly using the `CreateInstance()` method of the `Assembly` class. The `CreateInstance()` method has three overloaded implementations:

- ❑ `CreateInstance(typeName As String) As Object`

- ❑ `CreateInstance(typeName As String, ignoreCase as Boolean) as Object`

- ❑ `CreateInstance(typeName As String, ignoreCase as Boolean, bindingAttr as BindingFlags, binder as Binder, args as Object(), culture as CultureInfo, activationAttributes as Object()) As Object`

n the simplest case, the `CreateInstance()` method has one argument, which accepts a string that identifies the type to be loaded. The class name is case sensitive, unless the second parameter is set to `True`.

The third method gives the developer the most control over the creation of the instance of the class. The reflection library uses the binding flags to determine which methods to search through to find the object's constructor. The binding flags enumeration is used in many methods in the refection library, but only the following 2 flags are relevant and can be combined by using an OR in the argument:

- ❑ `BindingFlags.Public` – Search only public methods. This includes both instance and shared methods.

- ❑ `BindingFlags.Instance` – Search instance methods in any scope. An instance method requires an instance of the object to be created, while static methods declared with the `Shared` keyword to not require the class to be instantiated.

96

The `binder` argument is an object that the `BindingFlags` and `args` arguments use to determine the constructor. Passing NULL in this field results in the default binder being used.

The `args` argument is an object array that contains the arguments to pass into the constructor. The reflection runtime will search through all the constructors and call the one appropriate for that list of objects.

The `CultureInfo` object determines the cultural environment that governs the coercion of types on the argument array. This occurs when a type is converted to another in the argument that may require some cultural information. For example, if a string object is passed into a date parameter, the conversion of "7/9/02" will differ depending on the cultural context, since some cultures define that date as July 9th, while others is September 7th. Setting this value to `Nothing` will default the culture to the current thread's culture.

The `activationAttributes` argument is an array of objects that contain some activation attributes. The `UrlAttribute` object is an example of a parameter to the `CreateInstance()` method, which determines where activation will take place.

```
' Load the assembly from the reflection library with a partial
reference
partial = "DynamicAssembly"
oAssembly = System.Reflection.Assembly.LoadWithPartialName(partial)

' Load the assembly with a full reference,
' but using the LoadWithPartialName
partial = "DynamicAssembly, Version=1.0.950.28158, _
           Culture=neutral, PublicKeyToken=null"
oAssembly = System.Reflection.Assembly.LoadWithPartialName(partial)
```

The following is a trivial example that demonstrates how to load the assembly dynamically and create an instance of the class. First in a class library create a simple class with two constructors: a default constructor that takes in no arguments, and another constructor that takes in a `long` argument. It stores the argument in a private variable. We also create a method that returns that number.

```
Public Class CDynamicLoadedClass
   Sub New()
     m_lNumber = -1
   End Sub
   Sub New(ByVal lDefault As Long)
     m_lNumber = lDefault
   End Sub


   Public Function GetNumber() As Long
      Return m_lNumber
   End Function

   Private m_lNumber As Long
End Class
```

Now, create a simple windows form application that has a single command button on it. In the command button routine, we will place the code to dynamically load the object.

```
Private Sub Button1_Click(ByVal sender As System.Object, _
    ByVal e As System.EventArgs) Handles Button1.Click
  Dim oAssemblyName As System.Reflection.AssemblyName
  Dim oAssembly As System.Reflection.Assembly
  Dim oClass As DynamicAssembly.CDynamicLoadedClass
  Dim args(0) As Object


  ' Use the AssemblyName object
  oAssemblyName = New System.Reflection.AssemblyName()
  oAssemblyName.Name = "DynamicAssembly"
  oAssemblyName.Version = New Version("1.0.950.28158")
  oAssembly = System.Reflection.Assembly.Load(oAssemblyName)

  ' Since you are not passing in an args array,
  ' use the default constructor
  oClass = _
      oAssembly.CreateInstance("DynamicAssembly.CDynamicLoadedClass")
  MsgBox(oClass.GetNumber())
  oClass = Nothing

  ' Set up the args array.
  ' We will pass in 1 object with a datatype of Long
  args(0) = CLng(5)
  oClass = _
      oAssembly.CreateInstance("DynamicAssembly.CDynamicLoadedClass", _
      True, Nothing, Nothing, args, Nothing, Nothing)
  MsgBox(oClass.GetNumber())

End Sub
```

The result of this simple program is two message boxes. The first displays a value of –1 and the second displays a value of 5. This demonstrates which constructor was used in instantiating the object.

Abstract Factory Pattern

Dynamic assembly loading is a powerful tool provided by .NET, but in order to fully utilize it, a structure that organizes the logic to decide which assembly to load and object to instantiate without affecting the calling assembly must be created. The technique of centralizing object instantiation is not unique to .NET. Object oriented developers in languages such as C++ and Java use a construct called the **Abstract Factory Pattern**. This technique, like many common object-oriented architectures, derives from SmallTalk, and the Gamma et al book, *Design Patterns* (Addison Wesley, 1994, 0-201-63361-2). The authors of this book identified the abstract factory pattern as a way to provide a centralized location for the selection of a class to dynamically load. More information on how this and many other design patterns can be used in Visual Basic .NET can be found in *Professional Design Patterns in VB.NET*, published by Wrox (1-86100-698-5).

The abstract factory pattern allows a programmer to obtain an object matching a particular interface, but only choosing which specific class to instantiate at runtime. One of several possible classes could be instantiated, but whichever is returned, the calling code can treat the object the same because it implements a particular interface. The specific type of the returned object might be completely unknown to the calling code.

*The word abstract, in the context of the abstract factory pattern, refers to the fact that it is based upon an **abstract class**. Abstract classes, in OO parlance, are classes which declare only a partial implementation – they leave some of their methods with signatures, but no method body. They cannot be instantiated, but they can be subclassed, and the subclasses must provide a complete implementation for the class, filling in the missing methods. A class which inherits from an abstract class and completes the implementation is called a **concrete class**. In VB.NET, we can create an abstract class by marking it with the* `MustInherit` *keyword.*

Here's a diagram explaining what an abstract factory tries to do:

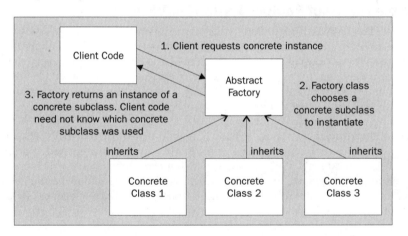

The implementation of the abstract factory pattern consists of implementing an abstract class, and some concrete classes which extend it. The client code, though, only has to know about the abstract factory class itself, and need not know about the concrete classes. This is because of polymorphism; an instance of any of the concrete classes can be referred from a variable whose type is that of the abstract factory class itself. So, although the abstract class itself can never be instantiated, instances of the subclasses can be treated, to all intents and purposes, as if they are instances of the abstract type. The client will make method calls on the concrete class through the interface provided by the abstract class.

99

Advantages of Using the Abstract Factory Pattern with Dynamic Assembly Loading

All this information about reflection, inheritance, and abstract factory patterns may seem interesting, but you may ask, how is this practical? Almost all of the examples in the chapter could be programmed without dynamic object creation, with a much simpler solution. Well, the power of dynamic assembly loading and object creation is its flexibility. The developer can design an architecture that can easily be expanded and extended without redevelopment, and in some cases can be added on the fly without recompiling the original source code. Imagine adding a module that handles a new set of electronic invoices, with new business rules and data transformations, to the existing data import program, without disturbing any of the original source code and without taking the system down. Although flexible software is more complex and there is a slight increase in overhead, which may hinder performance, the flexibility's benefits often outweigh the increased complexity and overhead. This is especially true in VB.NET, now that it is fully object oriented and can utilize inheritance.

A Simple Abstract Factory Pattern in VB.NET

An abstract class in .NET is identified by the MustInherit keyword. This means that the class cannot be created through a New keyword, but subclasses can inherit from the abstract class. The subclasses must implement methods declared in the abstract class to provide the underlying functionality. The abstract class supplies the interface that the clients communicate with, but also it can supply a set of generic methods and utility functions the concrete classes inherit.

In addition, the abstract class must provide a method that client code calls when it wants the factory to create a new instance for it. This can be implemented as a Shared method. This method may take arguments, which it can use to decide which concrete class to return, or it may not, using information found elsewhere to make the decision. In either case, it will be returning an instance of one of the concrete classes, so its return type will be the abstract factory's own type.

Following is a trivial example that shows how one could use an abstract factory pattern to display a greeting. The client of the factory has no knowledge of the NightGreeter, MorningGreeter or the other concrete classes, but rather uses the Greeter's GetGreeter() method to decide which concrete class is appropriate for the situation.

```
Public MustInherit Class Greeter

    Public Shared Function GetGreeter() As Greeter
        Dim now As DateTime = DateTime.Now
        Dim hour As Integer = now.Hour
        Dim currentGreeter As Greeter
```

```
      Select Case hour
        Case 0 To 6
          currentGreeter = New NightGreeter()
        Case 7 To 12
          currentGreeter = New MorningGreeter()
        Case 13 To 17
          currentGreeter = New AfternoonGreeter()
        Case Else
          currentGreeter = New EveningGreeter()
      End Select

      Return currentGreeter
    End Function

    Public MustOverride Function Greet() As String

End Class

Public Class MorningGreeter
  Inherits Greeter
  Public Overrides Function Greet() As String
    Return "Good morning"
  End Function
End Class

Public Class AfternoonGreeter
  Inherits Greeter
  Public Overrides Function Greet() As String
    Return "Good afternoon"
  End Function
End Class

Public Class EveningGreeter
  Inherits Greeter
  Public Overrides Function Greet() As String
    Return "Good evening"
  End Function
End Class

Public Class NightGreeter
  Inherits Greeter
  Public Overrides Function Greet() As String
    Return "What are you doing running this code at this hour?"
  End Function
End Class
```

Here's a trivial command-line client:

```
Public Module MainModule
  Public Sub Main()
    Dim g As Greeter = Greeter.GetGreeter()
    Console.WriteLine(g.Greet())
  End Sub
End Module
```

The output will now depend on the time of day. Notice how this pattern breaks up responsibility for different parts of the system neatly into logically distinct units; the logic of which greeting to deliver is all in the GetGreeting() method; the logic for each greeting is parceled up in a different class; the client code doesn't worry about how each different class implements the Greet() method, it just calls it. This is object-oriented encapsulation at its best.

So far so good, but we're not actually using reflection here. However, since the GetGreeting() method neatly encapsulates all of the logic that decides which object to create, it is easy for us to insert reflective code here, without affecting the implementation of the concrete classes, or the client code at all. Using reflective object loading, we can make the decision about which class to instantiate far more dynamic. For example, the application could read a configuration file to determine which class to use at any particular hour, using reflection to load the appropriate class. New greetings could be added simply by adding a new class to the application, and altering the configuration file. On Christmas Day, you could change the configuration file completely so that no matter what time the program is run, an instance of ChristmasGreeting is returned.

A more realistic business situation for the Abstract Factory Pattern is a data pipeline architecture. Data pipeline architectures push data through a series of processors that perform some operations on the data, such as transformations, database modifications and email notifications. A common application of a data pipeline would be an Enterprise Resource Planning (ERP) integration web service that a company exposes to communicate with vendors or customers. An ERP is an enterprise application that processes a wide range of business functions such as customer databases, accounting, and human resources. Typically, each node in a pipeline needs to discover another node to forward data onto after it has finished processing it. An abstract factory system would allow nodes to request other nodes by name, not worrying about the underlying type of the node which is returned, but still able to interact at a high level.

We'll look now at a real application of a dynamic assembly loading abstract factory, in a similar business workflow situation.

Implementing the Abstract Factory Pattern with Dynamic Assembly Loading in VB.NET

Let's examine a situation where we might apply these techniques.

A manufacturing company's accounting department wants to create an EDI (Electronic Data Interchange) invoicing and billing system. EDI systems are electronic connections to send information between the two companies electronically. In order to keep material costs low, the purchasing department wants as little barrier to switching suppliers as possible. Unfortunately, different vendors all use different systems for communication: email, FTP file drop, or more recently, XML web services. XML helps simplify some of the issues, but each vendor still needs individualized business rules applied to their incoming data.

The billing department also has similar concerns. In order to satisfy their customers, the sales team used numerous rebates and discounts as incentives. The billing system would have to be flexible enough to accommodate any customer demands on the contract terms. The software development team has found it impossible to create a data model to store all the possible contact terms in the database, since there are so many different possible contact terms possible.

We can implement this EDI system using a data pipeline that accommodates the various department's needs for flexibility, yet keeps the system manageable. The pipeline has 3 stages:

❑ Initial Transformation – Data is received via email, ftp, web service, etc in either a flat file or XML. It is then converted from the native format to an XML document. The transformation logic will be specific to each vendor's file format.

❑ Database load – Load the information into the ERP system after applying any special customer specific-logic.

❑ Notification – Some EDI vendors require electronic notification of receipt, and some internal departments require notification that an order has been shipped.

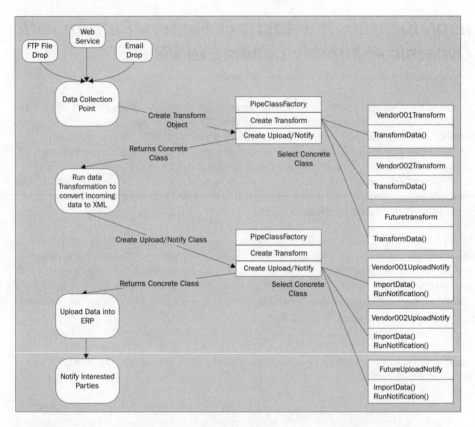

The pipeline uses a factory to load the assembly and component that processes the data as it flows through the pipeline. The factory class uses an XML file to store the assembly and class data, which allows new vendors to be added to the pipeline on the fly by coding up a new vendor-specific assembly, and editing the XML file. When an object is requested by the client, the factory queries the XML document and obtains the assembly identification data. The data is passed into the `Assembly.Load()` method to load the assembly, and the `CreateInstance()` method is called on the assembly object. The factory method is shared, which means that an instance of the class does not have to exist to call the method. The first time the shared method is called, the static constructor is run, which loads the XML document.

Let's look at the configuration document for the application first:

```xml
<?xml version="1.0" encoding="utf-8" ?>
<Pipeline>
  <vendor id="001">
    <assembly name="PipelineExample1" version="1.0">
      <class type="Transform"
```

```
          name="PipelineExample1.Vendor001Transform"/>
      <class type="UploadNotify"
          name="PipelineExample1.Vendor001UploadNotify"/>
    </assembly>
  </vendor>
  <vendor id="002">
    <assembly name="PipelineExample1" version="1.0">
      <class type="Transform"
          name="PipelineExample1.Vendor002Transform"/>
      <class type="UploadNotify"
          name="PipelineExample1.Vendor002UploadNotify"/>
    </assembly>
  </vendor>
</Pipeline>
```

As you can see, the file specifies for each vendor the name of a transformation and upload/notification class. The factory uses this to select the appropriate DLL to load, and class to use.

Here is the code for the factory class. It starts off with the shared constructor which loads the XML configuration file. It looks in the base directory for the current application domain, which means the configuration file must be in the directory containing the executable application which is currently running.

```
Public Class PipeLineClassFactory
    Private Shared _xmlDoc As Xml.XmlDocument

    Shared Sub New()
        _xmlDoc = New Xml.XmlDocument()
        ' NOTE- Hardcoding the filename is NOT recommended, but for
        ' the purposes of this example it will suffice.
        _xmlDoc.Load(AppDomain.CurrentDomain.BaseDirectory & _
                    "/pipelineconfig.xml")
    End Sub
```

The first of our factory methods creates a vendor-specific `Transform` object, from the vendor ID passed in:

```
Public Shared Function CreateTransform(ByVal vendorID As Long) _
                                As Transformation
    Dim xmlAssembly As Xml.XmlElement
    Dim xmlClass As Xml.XmlElement
    Dim name As String
    Dim version As String
    Dim className As String
    Dim args(0) As Object
    Dim assemblyName As System.Reflection.AssemblyName
    Dim loadedAssembly As System.Reflection.Assembly
    Dim ret As Transformation
```

```
' Load the data from the preloaded configuration XML Document
xmlAssembly = _xmlDoc.SelectSingleNode("/Pipeline/vendor[@id=" _
    & CStr(vendorID) & "]/assembly")
xmlClass = _
    xmlAssembly.SelectSingleNode("class[@type='Transform']")

' Pull out the assembly information from the Configuration
' File. This example uses a partial reference to load the assembly
' a full reference would include the culture and public key token
name = xmlAssembly.GetAttribute("name")
version = xmlAssembly.GetAttribute("version")
className = xmlClass.GetAttribute("name")

' Create and populate the AssemblyName object
assemblyName = New System.Reflection.AssemblyName()
assemblyName.Name = name
assemblyName.Version = New Version(version)

' Load the assembly from the reflection library
loadedAssembly = System.Reflection.Assembly.Load(assemblyName)
' The contructor takes no parameters
args = Nothing
' Create the instance of the class specified in the configuration
' file.
ret = loadedAssembly.CreateInstance(className, True, _
                Reflection.BindingFlags.Public Or _
                Reflection.BindingFlags.Instance, _
                Nothing, args, Nothing, Nothing)
Return ret

End Function
```

The next function is the factory that creates the vendor-specific upload and notification object, which is mostly the same, but requires an argument for the constructor.

```
Public Shared Function CreateUploadNotify(ByVal vendorID As Long, _
            ByVal xmlInvoice As Xml.XmlDocument) As UploadNotify
    Dim xmlAssembly As Xml.XmlElement
    Dim xmlClass As Xml.XmlElement
    Dim name As String
    Dim version As String
    Dim className As String
    Dim args(0) As Object

    Dim assemblyName As System.Reflection.AssemblyName
    Dim loadedAssembly As System.Reflection.Assembly
    Dim ret As UploadNotify

    xmlAssembly = _xmlDoc.SelectSingleNode("/Pipeline/vendor[@id=" _
            & CStr(vendorID) & "]/assembly")
    xmlClass = _
        xmlAssembly.SelectSingleNode("class[@type='UploadNotify']")
```

```
        name = xmlAssembly.GetAttribute("name")
        version = xmlAssembly.GetAttribute("version")
        className = xmlClass.GetAttribute("name")

        assemblyName = New System.Reflection.AssemblyName()
        assemblyName.Name = name
        assemblyName.Version = New Version(version)

        loadedAssembly = System.Reflection.Assembly.Load(assemblyName)

        ' The XmlInvoice parameter is the argument to the constructor
        args(0) = xmlInvoice
        ret = loadedAssembly.CreateInstance(className, True, _
                    Reflection.BindingFlags.Public And _
                    Reflection.BindingFlags.Instance, _
                    Nothing, args, Nothing, Nothing)
        Return ret

    End Function

End Class
```

The abstract classes in the data pipeline define the interface that the pipeline uses to pass the data along the pipeline. They also provide a default implementation that the subclass can override when the vendor requires special treatment. Lastly, the abstract base classes provide a set of utility functions that the subclasses can utilize to reuse code in common situations.

The first class handles transformation of data into the appropriate internal format. Here's an example of the XML format that the system requires:

```
<?xml version="1.0" encoding="utf-8" ?>
<Invoice VendorID="001" ProductName="WidgetComponent1"
        ProductID="212" Price=".02" Quantity="12500">
</Invoice>
```

Additional vendor-specific data is allowed, if the vendor wishes to supply it, in the form of additional XML attributes.

The base data transformation class caters for the case where the vendor sends invoices in the desired XML format, and they therefore require no transformation. The data will simply be loaded into an XML document and returned to the caller. Some vendors may send the file in a comma-delimited format, which would need to be parsed and loaded into an XML document before the method completes. You may also want to include some utility functions to help import some commonly used file formats.

```
Public MustInherit Class Transformation
  Public Overridable Function TransformData(ByVal data As String) _
                   As Xml.XmlDocument
    ' The default behavior is that the data provider
    ' sends the data in an XML format that
    ' conforms to the rules of the internal XML schema
    Dim xmlDoc As Xml.XmlDocument

    xmlDoc = New Xml.XmlDocument()
    ' You will want to provide error handling to
    ' ensure data loaded correctly.
    xmlDoc.LoadXml(data)

    Return xmlDoc
  End Function
End Class
```

The upload and notify class constructor uses reflection to look at the implementing subclass's public properties. For each property, it checks the XML document for a value to assign. If there is a match between the public property's name and a field in the XML file, the field is populated with the value. Properties are provided on the abstract class for the three compulsory fields that must be provided for an invoice, but this mechanism allows our code to process data from other vendors which provide additional information. Once again, extensibility is the goal.

```
Public MustInherit Class UploadNotify

  Public Sub New(ByVal xmlDoc As Xml.XmlDocument)
    Dim myType As Type
    Dim myPropertyInfos As PropertyInfo()
    Dim myPropertyInfo As PropertyInfo
    Dim xmlElt As Xml.XmlElement
    Dim i As Integer

    myType = Me.GetType()
    myPropertyInfos = myType.GetProperties()

    For Each myPropertyInfo In myPropertyInfos
      xmlElt = xmlDoc.SelectSingleNode("/Invoice[@" & _
          myPropertyInfo.Name & "]")
      myPropertyInfo.SetValue(Me, _
          CStr(xmlElt.GetAttribute(CStr(myPropertyInfo.Name))), _
          Nothing)
    Next
  End Sub
```

The two public methods that are called on an upload/notification class are next. First, the notification method:

```
Public Overridable Sub RunNotification()
    ' The base case in no notification, do nothing
End Sub
```

Here are some utility functions – the implementation is left out and we just post a message to the screen.

```
Protected Sub SendEmail(ByVal name As String, _
                ByVal emailAddr As String, _
                ByVal subject As String, _
                ByVal body As String)

    MsgBox(String.Format("Sending mail '{0}' to {1} ({2})", _
                subject, name, emailAddr))
End Sub

Protected Sub SendFax(ByVal name As String, _
                ByVal faxNbr As String, _
                ByVal subject As String, _
                ByVal body As String)

    MsgBox(String.Format("Sending fax '{0}' to {1} ({2})", _
                subject, name, faxNbr))
End Sub
```

The other key public method is called to import the data into the ERP system. The `ImportData()` method of the `UploadNotify` class creates the connection to the ERP system and loads the data in. The implementation of this varies greatly from one system to another, so the specific implementation of this functionality is omitted in this example. One possible way to import the data is to pass a SQL statement to the database and insert the data directly. This may not be possible in a real system, as many ERPs lock the database down so modifications must be made through ERP's import API, but it suffices to show what we're doing here.

We provide a default implementation here, but expect that vendor-specific logic might be required, so allow this implementation to be overridden. We call one method that generates an appropriate SQL statement, and another that executes it against our ERP database.

```
Public Overridable Sub ImportData()
    ' The base case is to just create the SQL insert statement
    ' dynamically and run the query in the DB.
    Dim sql As String

    sql = GenerateSQL()
    ExecuteSQL(sql)
End Sub
```

109

The SQL generation logic again uses reflection to examine the properties exposed by the current implementing class, and builds a SQL statement using them.

```
Friend Function GenerateSQL()
   Dim sql As String
   Dim myType As Type
   Dim myPropertyInfos As PropertyInfo()
   Dim myPropertyInfo As PropertyInfo
   Dim xmlElt As Xml.XmlElement
   Dim i As Integer

   myType = Me.GetType()
   myPropertyInfos = myType.GetProperties()
   sql = "INSERT INTO AcctPayable ("
   For Each myPropertyInfo In myPropertyInfos
      sql = sql & myPropertyInfo.Name & ", "
   Next
   sql = sql.Substring(0, sql.Length - 2) ' Remove trailing comma
                                          ' and space
   sql = sql & ") VALUES ("

   For Each myPropertyInfo In myPropertyInfos
      sql = sql & "'" & myPropertyInfo.GetValue(Me, Nothing) & "', "
   Next
   sql = sql.Substring(0, sql.Length - 2) ' Remove trailing comma
                                          ' and space
   sql = sql & ")"

   Return sql
End Function
```

The next sub would execute the generated SQL query, but in our demonstration, it just shows it to the user using a message box.

```
Friend Sub ExecuteSQL(ByVal sql As String)
   MsgBox("Executing SQL Statement " & sql)
End Sub
```

Finally, we have the three properties that are required for every invoice.

```
Private _productID As String
Private _price As String
Private _quantity As String

' Required Field Names
Public Property ProductID() As String
   Get
      Return _productID
   End Get
```

```
      Set(ByVal Value As String)
         _productID = Value
      End Set
   End Property

   Public Property Price() As String
      Get
         Return _price
      End Get
      Set(ByVal Value As String)
         _price = Value
      End Set
   End Property

   Public Property Quantity() As String
      Get
         Return _quantity
      End Get
      Set(ByVal Value As String)
         _quantity = Value
      End Set
   End Property

End Class
```

Now we need to implement the actual vendor-specific classes. Suppose this is Vendor 001's first EDI interchange project, and they are willing to send their data in the desired XML format. This means that no transformation is required. The concrete `Transform` class created for Vendor 001 will not override the `Transform()` method and will default to the implementation provided by the abstract class.

```
Public Class Vendor001Transform
   ' Vendor 001 agreed to use XYZ's internal layout, so no
   ' initial transformation must be done
   Inherits Transformation

End Class
```

However, on the notification side, Vendor 001 provides an additional shipping date field in the XML file it passes to the EDI web service. The loading dock's manager might use this shipping field to help plan his workload since he will know roughly when shipments are due to arrive. The notification section of the pipeline needs to send an email out to him when the data is received. This is done by overriding the `RunNotification()` method of the `UploadNotify` class, and by adding a `ShipDate` public property to the subclass. Remember, the constructor in the base class must be called using the `MyBase.New()` function, which will automatically set the new property from the data in the XML.

111

```
Public Class Vendor001UploadNotify
  Inherits UploadNotify

  Private _shipDate As String

  Public Sub New(ByVal xmlDoc As System.Xml.XmlDocument)
    MyBase.New(xmlDoc)
  End Sub

  Public Property ShipDate() As String
    Get
      Return _shipDate
    End Get
    Set(ByVal Value As String)
      _shipDate = Value
    End Set
  End Property

  ' Once again, the hard coded email address is not recommended,
  ' but simply demonstrates what data could be sent.
  Public Overrides Sub RunNotification()
    Me.SendEmail("Loading Docks Manager", _
                 "ldmgr@CompanyXYZ.com", _
                 "Shipment from Vender 001", _
                 "Shipping date: " & _shipDate)
  End Sub

End Class
```

Now, suppose Vendor 002 has been using EDI for quite some time and is unwilling to rewrite their existing EDI system to accommodate XML. Instead, their data is sent via a flat file to an FTP server. A process then watches for files being uploaded, and loads them into the pipeline server. The data within the flat file is comma delimited, with one row per line. The data must be parsed and loaded into an XML document before it can be passed onto the next stage in the pipeline system. By overriding the TransformData() method of the Transform class, the class can perform this data transformation without having to change the architecture and dataflow through the rest of the system.

Here is an example of the Vendor 002 invoice Format:

```
"Product","Price","Quantity","Ship-Date"
"WidgetComponent2","0.02","456","06/13/2002"
```

We need to turn this data into an XML file matching the format specified before – an <invoice> element, with the data stored as attributes. Here's how we do that:

```
' Vendor 002 uses a flat comma delimited file format for all EDI.
Public Class Vendor002Transform
  Inherits Transformation
```

```
Public Overrides Function TransformData(ByVal data As String) _
            As Xml.XmlDocument
  ' Parse the data sent in via the CSV
  Dim xmlDoc As Xml.XmlDocument
  Dim invoice As Xml.XmlElement

  xmlDoc = New Xml.XmlDocument()
  xmlDoc.LoadXml("<Invoice/>")

  invoice = xmlDoc.DocumentElement

  Dim lines As String()
  Dim line As String
  Dim fields As String()
  Dim field As String
  Dim header As Boolean
  data = data.Replace("""", "") ' remove quotes
  lines = data.Split(vbCrLf) ' split into lines
  header = True
  For Each line In lines
    If header Then
      header = False ' omit the first line
    Else
      fields = line.Split(",") ' split on commas
      invoice.SetAttribute("VendorID", "002")
      invoice.SetAttribute("ProductID", _
            ConvertProductNameToID(fields(0).Trim()))
      invoice.SetAttribute("Price", fields(1))
      invoice.SetAttribute("Quantity", fields(2))
      invoice.SetAttribute("EstimatedArrivalDate", fields(3))
    End If

  Next

  Return xmlDoc
End Function

Private Function ConvertProductNameToID( _
        ByVal productName As String) As String
  Select Case productName
    Case "WidgetComponent1"
      Return "212"
    Case "WidgetComponent2"
      Return "213"
  End Select
End Function

End Class
```

Unlike Vendor 001 however, no notifications are required, so we accept the default behavior. We must implement a constructor, however, so the XML document passed in is correctly stored and uploaded into the ERP system by the base class.

```
Public Class Vendor002UploadNotify
  Inherits UploadNotify
```

```
Public Sub New(ByVal xmlDoc As Xml.XmlDocument)
   MyBase.New(xmlDoc)
End Sub

End Class
```

Coding a client application isn't too difficult. For a quick demonstration, we can build a fast Windows program. Drag a textbox, a couple of buttons, and a listbox onto a form. The textbox should be multiline enabled. Change the caption on Button1 to **Process Vendor File**, and on Button2 to **Browse...**. Add the two strings `001` and `002` to the listbox. With a pair of labels added, here's what the form should look like:

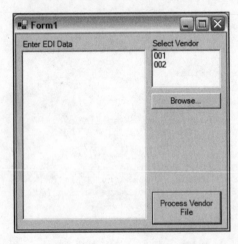

Add an `OpenFileDialog` component to the form as well, and switch to code view. We just need to handle clicks on the two buttons. First, the **Browse...** button, which we'll use to let the user load a vendor's EDI file into the text box (you can type it in, but a file-based import is useful):

```
Private Sub Button2_Click(ByVal sender As System.Object, _
            ByVal e As System.EventArgs) Handles Button2.Click
   Dim result As DialogResult
   Dim fileReader As System.IO.StreamReader

   result = OpenFileDialog1.ShowDialog()

   If result = DialogResult.OK Then
      fileReader = _
         New System.IO.StreamReader(OpenFileDialog1.FileName)
      TextBox1.Text = fileReader.ReadToEnd
      fileReader.Close()
   End If

End Sub
```

Next, the Process Vendor File button, which uses the pipeline system to import the data.

```
Private Sub Button1_Click(ByVal sender As System.Object, _
        ByVal e As System.EventArgs) Handles Button1.Click
    Dim transformer As PipeLineExample1.Transformation
    Dim uploadNotifier As PipeLineExample1.UploadNotify

    Dim xmlDoc As Xml.XmlDocument

    transformer = _
        PipeLineExample1.PipeLineClassFactory.CreateTransform( _
            ListBox1.SelectedItem)

    xmlDoc = transformer.TransformData(TextBox1.Text)

    uploadNotifier = _
        PipeLineExample1.PipeLineClassFactory.CreateUploadNotify( _
            ListBox1.SelectedItem, xmlDoc)

    uploadNotifier.ImportData()
    uploadNotifier.RunNotification()

End Sub
```

Now, enter either an XML formatted file from Vendor 001, or a comma-delimited Vendor 002 file, select the vendor ID from the list, and hit the button. A series of message boxes should display showing that processing is progressing.

Summary

By joining the abstract factory pattern concept and dynamic assembly loading and object creation in VB.NET, a developer can create a highly flexible and extendable application. Dynamic Assembly loading allows new assemblies to be loaded into an application, even after the application has been compiled. The abstract factory pattern centralizes the decision logic for which concrete instance of an object should be created given the parameters sent into the factory class. Although these structures add some complexity to the code, this increase in complexity is often outweighed by the flexibility gained, especially in situations where the system requirements are constantly changing.

VB.NET

Reflection

Handbook

5

5

Attributes

We've seen how reflection allows us to examine objects, determine their type, and access metadata the compiler places in the compiled type that tells us the names of its members, the signatures of its methods, and so on. We can discover in this way a great deal about the object, and how we can interact with it. But this might not be all we want to know about a type, especially when we're manipulating it reflectively. We might have a routine that can take any object, and create a dialog box with text boxes that allow us to manipulate its properties. But then some properties might not be suitable for manipulation in this way – how can the programmer of a class let this dialog box code know that a particular property should be ignored? We need to add additional metadata to the type, which the dialog box generator can examine to determine whether or not to add an entry for each property. .NET provides a mechanism for us to add such custom metadata, through the system of attributes.

The concept of metadata harks back to Artificial Intelligence research in the 1960s and 1970s, when it was first recognized that computers needed to have data about data in order to manipulate it. We've come a long way since then; the .NET Framework relies fundamentally on metadata to load and run applications in the common language runtime.

Attributes provide a standard and extensible way for .NET programmers to insert additional metadata into their assemblies. This metadata can be inspected by the common language runtime, to determine how to load and run a .NET application, by classes in the .NET Framework to determine how to manipulate objects, and by our own code. There are also attributes that are understood by compilers, and which modify the way the code is compiled. Effectively, attributes provide an escape mechanism from the syntax of our chosen programming language, enabling us to provide active information about the assemblies, types, fields, methods and so on in our code, to any other piece of code that is interested in them.

Attributes pave the way for an entirely new style of programming, often referred to as "aspect oriented programming". Developers can use attributes to declaratively annotate their assemblies, type definitions, methods, properties, and fields with additional aspects of behavior. For example, we can use attributes to indicate whether transactions are required on a type, whether a method can be invoked as a Web Service method, and whether a particular field is serializable. We can also use attributes to gain direct access to the Windows API; to mark methods as obsolete or conditionally compiled; to control the XML serialization format for objects; and much more besides.

When we use attributes in our code, the compiler injects "attribute objects" into the compiled MSIL code. These attribute objects inform the code which encounters instances of our types to provide the requested service, without requiring us to write any additional procedural code. For example, if we use an attribute to indicate that a data type requires transactions, and pass an object of this type to a library that provides transaction support for objects that request it, this library will provide the transactional logic on our behalf; we do not need to write any procedural code to create or manage transactions.

So, what exactly is an attribute? An attribute is a specialized class that inherits from System.Attribute, and allows the programmer to attach extra meaning to their code. As we move through this chapter, we'll look at a variety of examples that illustrate how to use existing attribute classes defined in the .NET Framework class library. We'll also see how to define new attribute classes of our own, and discuss why this might be a useful thing to do.

As well as being able to define and use attributes, we can also use reflection to access the attributes defined on an assembly, a type, a method, or a field. For example, we can use reflection to ascertain the version number and title of an assembly, establish whether a type is serializable, determine whether a type is visible to COM clients, and so on. Reflection allows us to write very smart code to interrogate the full capabilities of the coding elements in our application.

Here's a roadmap for the chapter:

❑ First, we'll introduce the essential syntax for using attributes in Visual Basic .NET. We'll see how to annotate a class definition with attributes, in order to inform the world that the class should support a particular feature. As a concrete example, we'll see how to use SerializableAttribute to indicate that a class is serializable.

We'll also see how to use attributes on specific fields within a class. For example, we'll show how to use NonSerializedAttribute to exclude specific fields from serialization in a serializable class.

❑ Once we've tackled the syntactic issues, we'll take a detailed look at a variety of existing attribute classes in the .NET Framework class library. For example, we'll see how to use the `ConditionalAttribute` attribute class to define conditionally-compiled methods. This enables us to define additional context for our code; for instance, we can clearly differentiate between debug code and release code in an application. This technique can be particularly helpful when we develop large-scale applications, because we don't have to comment out our diagnostic code; we can simply annotate diagnostic code with `ConditionalAttribute`.

Another important use of attribute classes is to define metadata for an entire assembly. For example, we can define the assembly's name, version, public key token, and culture information. These assembly attributes allow us to create strongly named assemblies, which in turn enables us to insert the assemblies into the global assembly cache. We'll investigate all these issues during the chapter.

❑ The final section of the chapter discusses the rules for defining new attribute classes, and shows how to use reflection to retrieve the custom attributes defined on a target.

Before we delve into the details, let's take some time out to explore the syntax for defining and using attribute classes.

Understanding Attributes

The best way to understand attributes is to take a look at some of the existing attribute classes in the .NET Framework class library. The following table introduces some of the most commonly used attribute classes in .NET:

Attribute class name	Description
`System.SerializableAttribute`	Marks a type (such as a class or structure) as being serializable. This means the fields in the type can be serialized to SOAP or binary format, to allow instances of this type to be passed across .NET remoting boundaries.
	If you do not require a type to be serializable, omit this attribute when you define the type; the default behavior is non-serializable.

Table continued on following page

Attribute class name	Description
System.NonSerializedAttribute	When you serialize an instance of a serializable type, all the fields in the instance will be serialized by default.
	There are some occasions where you might not want to serialize particular fields. For example, there is no point serializing fields that are specific to the original context of execution, such as a thread ID or a window handle obtained from a Win32 API call.
	To indicate that a specific field in a serializable type should not be serialized, annotate the field with NonSerializedAttribute.
System.Web.Services. WebServiceAttribute	This attribute provides additional information about a web service class, such as the XML namespace for the web service.
	By default, Visual Studio .NET generates the XML namespace "http://tempuri.org/" for web service classes.
System.Web.Services. WebMethodAttribute	This attribute indicates that a method in a web service class is a web service method.
	If you do not annotate a method with this attribute, the method will not be exposed as a web service method.
System.Reflection. AssemblyVersionAttribute	This attribute defines a version number for an assembly. This enables applications to bind to a specific version of an assembly.
	By default, Visual Studio .NET generates the version number 1.0.* for each assembly. The * is a wildcard character, which allows the compiler to choose an appropriate build number and revision for the assembly.
System.Diagnostics. ConditionalAttribute	This attribute indicates to the compiler that the method should only be compiled if a particular preprocessor identifier has been defined.
	Methods that are not annotated with this attribute are always compiled unconditionally.

Notice that all of the standard attribute classes in the .NET Framework end with 'Attribute'. This is only a convention, but it's a very strong convention. We'll follow this convention when we define our own custom attribute classes later in this chapter.

Also, each attribute class can be used in conjunction with a particular type (or group of types). For example:

❏ SerializableAttribute can be applied to classes, structures, enums, and delegates. SerializableAttribute cannot be applied to other kinds of coding element, such as interfaces, methods, constructors, or fields.

❏ NonSerializedAttribute can only be applied to fields.

❏ WebServiceAttribute can only be applied to classes.

❏ WebMethodAttribute can only be applied to methods.

❏ AssemblyVersionAttribute can only be applied to assemblies.

❏ ConditionalAttribute can only be applied to methods.

You should also have spotted that each attribute class is used for a specific purpose. For example:

❏ SerializableAttribute and NonSerializedAttribute are used by the common language runtime to control serialization and deserialization of objects.

❏ WebServiceAttribute and WebMethodAttribute are used by ASP.NET to facilitate web services.

❏ AssemblyVersionAttribute is used by the common language runtime to identify which version of an assembly should be loaded.

❏ ConditionalAttribute is used by the compiler to decide whether a method should be compiled or ignored.

Later in the chapter, when we write our own custom attributes, we'll see how to use attributes for our own purposes. But it's important to realize that the power of an attribute doesn't come from applying it, but from the code that looks to see if it's there, and changes its behavior accordingly. In other words, coding attributes alone isn't worthwhile, without also coding up a method that looks for them and varies its actions accordingly.

Obviously, many of the methods developed by the Microsoft developers who created the .NET framework classes use attributes.

Syntax for Using Attributes

To illustrate the syntax for using attributes, we'll take a look at a simple Visual Basic .NET application that defines a serializable class named `Account`. The application will create an `Account` object and serialize it to an XML document in the Simple Object Access Protocol (SOAP) format.

> *SOAP is an XML-based protocol for invoking methods across the Internet, and for passing simple and structured data as parameters and return values for these methods. The SOAP protocol is defined by the World Wide Web Consortium (W3C). The latest version of the SOAP protocol, version 1.2, is currently still at the Working Draft stage at the time of writing; for a very readable introduction, see* http://www.w3c.org/TR/soap12-part0/.

Our sample application also shows how to deserialize SOAP data held in an XML document, to reconstitute the `Account` object in memory. You can download the source code for this example from `ch05\SerializationDemo.vb` in the download folder for this book.

To kick off, the application requires three `Imports` statements as follows:

```
Imports System
Imports System.IO
Imports System.Runtime.Serialization.Formatters.Soap
```

These three namespaces provide the following functionality:

- ❑ The `System` namespace contains the `SerializableAttribute` and `NonSerializedAttribute` classes, which we'll use to specify the serialization capabilities of our `Account` class.

- ❑ The `System.IO` namespace contains the standard file I/O classes in .NET.

- ❑ The `System.Runtime.Serialization.Formatters.Soap` namespace contains the `SoapFormatter` class, which we'll use to perform the serialization and deserialization of our `Account` object.

Now let's define the `Account` class as a serializable class. Here is the code for the class, with the serialization aspects highlighted:

```
<SerializableAttribute()> _
Public Class Account

  ' These fields will be serialized
  Private mName As String
  Private mBalance As Double
```

```
' This (rather contrived) field will not be serialized
<NonSerializedAttribute()> _
Private mMachineName As String

' Constructor
Public Sub New(ByVal Name As String)
  mName = Name
  mBalance = 0.0
End Sub

' Deposit funds
Public Sub Deposit(ByVal Amount As Double)
  mBalance += Amount
End Sub

' Withdraw funds
Public Sub Withdraw(ByVal Amount As Double)
  mBalance -= Amount
End Sub

' Property to get the machine name (lazy initialization)
Public ReadOnly Property MachineName() As String
  Get
    If mMachineName Is Nothing Then
      mMachineName = Environment.MachineName
    End If
    Return mMachineName
  End Get
End Property

' Return object's state as a string
Public Overrides Function ToString() As String
  Return mName & ", $" & mBalance & ", machine name " & MachineName
End Function

End Class
```

Note the following points in the Account class:

❑   The Account class is annotated with the <SerializableAttribute()>
    attribute, which means Account is a serializable class. The angled brackets
    <> are Visual Basic .NET syntax for an attribute block.

*Visual C# and Managed Extensions for C++ use square brackets rather
than angled brackets for attribute blocks. For example, the syntax for
using SerializableAttribute in these languages is
[SerializableAttribute].*

❑   An attribute block can contain any number of attributes, separated by
    commas. In the Account example above, we've just defined a single
    attribute, SerializableAttribute. In the following example, we use a
    pair of attributes to indicate the class is both serializable and transactional:

```
Imports System                    ' For SerializableAttribute class
Imports System.EnterpriseServices ' For TransactionAttribute class

<SerializableAttribute(),TransactionAttribute()> _
Public Class MyAwesomeClass
   ' Members ...
End Class
```

❑   The empty parentheses () after an attribute declaration indicate that the
    attribute doesn't require any initialization arguments. Later in the chapter,
    we'll see examples of attributes that do require initialization arguments in
    the parentheses.

❑   The mMachineName field in our Account class is annotated with
    <NonSerializedAttribute()>, which means mMachineName should be
    ignored when Account objects are serialized and deserialized. The
    purpose of the mMachineName field is to hold the name of the local
    computer; this field is initialized the first time it is requested, in the
    MachineName property procedure. There is no point in serializing this
    field, because the chances are the object will be deserialized on a different
    computer. For example, if we pass an Account object to a remoting
    application, the object will be serialized on our computer and then
    deserialized on the server computer (which has a different name).

❑   The Account class has additional methods, a constructor, and a MachineName
    property procedure, to provide simple bank account functionality.

> **When we use attributes in our code, Visual Basic .NET allows
> us to omit the 'Attribute' part at the end of attribute names.
> For example, we can specify <Serializable()> rather than
> <SerializableAttribute()>. The class is still named
> SerializableAttribute, it's just that when we use the
> attribute, the compiler allows us to use the abbreviated
> name, Serializable. When using attributes, it's common
> practice to use the abbreviated syntax rather than the full
> attribute name, so we'll adopt this approach from now on in
> this chapter.**

Let's continue with our sample application, located in SerializationDemo.vb. The
following code shows how to serialize an Account object to SOAP format, using a
SoapFormatter object; the serialized data is written to an XML file named
AccountData.xml. The example also shows how to deserialize the data from this
XML file, to recreate an Account object in memory:

```
Public Class TestSerialization

  Public Shared Sub Main()
    MySerialize("AccountData.xml")
    MyDeserialize("AccountData.xml")
  End Sub

    Public Shared Sub MySerialize(ByVal FileName As String)

        ' Create an Account object, and perform some transactions
        Dim acc1 As New Account("Jayne")
        acc1.Deposit(3000)
        acc1.Withdraw(1000)
        Console.WriteLine("Object state: {0}", acc1)

        ' Use a SoapFormatter to serialize the Account object
        Dim stream As FileStream = File.Create(FileName)
        Dim formatter As New SoapFormatter()
        Console.Write("Serializing object... ")
        formatter.Serialize(stream, acc1)
        stream.Close()

        Console.WriteLine("done.")

    End Sub

    Private Shared Sub MyDeserialize(ByVal FileName As String)

        ' Use a SoapFormatter to deserialize data
        Dim stream As FileStream = File.OpenRead(FileName)
        Dim formatter As New SoapFormatter()
        Console.Write("Deserializing object... ")
        Dim acc1 As Account = CType(formatter.Deserialize(stream), _
                                     Account)
        stream.Close()

        Console.WriteLine("done.")
        Console.WriteLine("Object state: {0}", acc1)

    End Sub

End Class
```

*The .NET Framework also allows us to serialize objects in binary format,
using the* `BinaryFormatter` *class rather than* `SoapFormatter`. *Binary
serialization is more memory-efficient than SOAP serialization, which can
be an important issue if we want to pass objects to remote methods across
a network. However, note that binary serialization only works if the
recipient application is written in .NET, because binary serialization uses
a proprietary format that is only recognized by .NET applications. To use
binary serialization, import the namespace*
`System.Runtime.Serialization.Formatters.Binary`, *and replace
all occurrences of* `SoapFormatter` *in the code with* `BinaryFormatter`.

To examine the metadata for our application, navigate a command prompt window to the directory containing the compiled code, and type the following command to run the MSIL Disassembler. The /adv switch runs the MSIL Disassembler in advanced mode, which offers us a great deal of additional information about the compiled code:

```
> ildasm /adv SerializationDemo.exe
```

The MSIL Disassembler window displays the following information for the Account class:

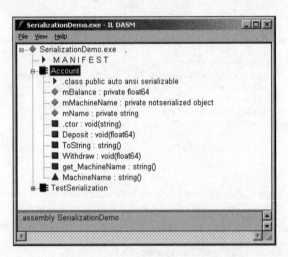

Notice the following points in the MSIL Disassembler window:

❑   The Account class is qualified as **serializable**, because we annotated this class with <SerializableAttribute()> in our code.

❑   The mMachineName field is qualified as **notserialized**, because we annotated this field with <NonSerializedAttribute()> in our code.

To obtain more detailed metadata, select the menu command View | MetaInfo | Show! in the MSIL Disassembler window. Another window appears, displaying the following information; we've highlighted the relevant parts:

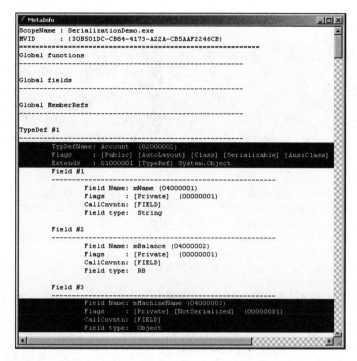

```
MetaInfo                                                              _ |□| x|
ScopeName : SerializationDemo.exe
MVID      : {30B501DC-CB84-4173-A22A-CB5AAF2246CB}
=================================================================
Global functions
-----------------------------------------------------------------

Global fields
-----------------------------------------------------------------

Global MemberRefs
-----------------------------------------------------------------

TypeDef #1
-----------------------------------------------------------------
        TypDefName: Account   (02000002)
        Flags     : [Public] [AutoLayout] [Class] [Serializable] [AnsiClass]
        Extends   : 01000001 [TypeRef] System.Object
        Field #1
        ---------------------------------------------------------
                Field Name: mName (04000001)
                Flags     : [Private]   (00000001)
                CallCnvntn: [FIELD]
                Field type: String

        Field #2
        ---------------------------------------------------------
                Field Name: mBalance (04000002)
                Flags     : [Private]   (00000001)
                CallCnvntn: [FIELD]
                Field type: R8

        Field #3
        ---------------------------------------------------------
                Field Name: mMachineName (04000003)
                Flags     : [Private] [NotSerialized]   (00000081)
                CallCnvntn: [FIELD]
                Field type: Object
```

Notice the following points:

❑   The metadata for the `Account` class includes the [Serializable] flag, to
    indicate to the common language runtime that this is a serializable class.
    Later in this section, we'll show how to use reflection to interrogate an
    object for its attributes.

❑   The metadata for the `mMachineName` field includes the [NotSerialized] flag,
    to indicate to the common language runtime that this field should not be
    serialized or deserialized.

It's worth noting here that the serialization capabilities of our type are listed under the
heading of `Flags`, along with such information as the accessibility modifier (`Private` or
`Public`). These are all regarded as 'standard attributes' in .NET, and obviously we apply
many of them using language keywords. Where the language doesn't provide a keyword
(note VBNET's lack of a `Serializable` keyword) .NET provides us with an attribute,
which the compiler interprets, inserting the appropriate flags into the IL metadata.

Custom attributes such as those we write ourselves, many of which are also defined in
the .NET class libraries, are included in the metadata, but inside a slightly different flag.

To run the application, type the following command:

```
> SerializationDemo.exe
```

The application displays the following messages on the console:

```
Visual Studio .NET Command Prompt
C:\Reflection\ch05>SerializationDemo.exe
Object state: Jayne, $2000, machine name MYCOMPUTERNAME
Serializing object... done.
Deserializing object... done.
Object state: Jayne, $2000, machine name MYCOMPUTERNAME

C:\Reflection\ch05>
```

The first two messages on the console indicate the initial state of the object, before it is serialized to the XML document. The final two messages indicate the state of the object that is deserialized from the XML document. Note that the machine name information isn't serialized or deserialized; when we display the MachineName property using the deserialized object, the machine name is recalculated on the current machine. Our sample application serializes and deserializes the data on the same machine, so we happen to see the same machine name (MYCOMPUTERNAME) before and after serialization.

To prove that the machine name information isn't serialized, open AccountData.xml in Internet Explorer. The document appears as follows:

```
Visual Studio .NET Command Prompt
C:\Reflection\ch05>SerializationDemo.exe
Object state: Jayne, $2000, machine name MYCOMPUTERNAME
Serializing object... done.
Deserializing object... done.
Object state: Jayne, $2000, machine name MYCOMPUTERNAME

C:\Reflection\ch05>
```

AccountData.xml is a SOAP document. SOAP documents begin with a <SOAP-ENV:Envelope> root element, and have a <SOAP-ENV:Body> element containing the actual information. We won't discuss the SOAP-related content of the document here, because we're more interested in .NET attributes than SOAP nuances. For more information about the use of SOAP in .NET, see *Professional XML for .NET Developers*, ISBN 1-86100-531-8, published by Wrox Press.

Notice the following points inside the <SOAP-ENV:Body> element:

❑ The <a1:Account> element contains the serialized data for our Account object. a1 is a namespace prefix for the following namespace URL, which specifies details for the assembly that contains the Account class. We'll see how to use .NET attributes to specify an assembly's name, version, culture, and public key token later in this chapter. The common language runtime uses this information during deserialization, to identify the assembly in which the Account class is defined. This enables the runtime to load the required assembly into memory, to gain access to the Account class definition:

```
"http://schemas.microsoft.com/clr/assem/SerializationDemo%2C%20
Version%3D0.0.0.0%2C%20Culture%3Dneutral%2C%20PublicKeyToken%3Dnull"
```

❑ The <Account> element has an id="ref-1" XML attribute. When we serialize a reference-type object, such as an instance of the Account class, the serialization mechanism generates a unique ID number for the object. Each time we perform serialization, every serialized object has a unique ID within the serialized document. This enables us to serialize objects that contain reference to other objects; the serialization mechanism uses the object's ID numbers to remember which objects refer to which other objects.

❑ The <Account> element has child elements named <mName> and <mBalance>, which contain the values of the serializable fields in our Account object. Notice that <mName> has a reference number, because the mName field is a reference type (String); however, <mBalance> does not have a reference number, because the mBalance field is a value type (double).

❑ The serialized document does not have an element named <mMachineName>, because we annotated the mMachineName field with the <NonSerializedAttribute()> .NET attribute.

Testing a Data Type for Standard Attributes

As we've just shown in the previous section, the <Serializable()> attribute marks a type as serializable. When we try to serialize an object in our application, the common language runtime inspects the metadata for the object's type, to see if the type is serializable. If we try to serialize an unserializable type, the runtime will detect this error condition and throw a
System.Runtime.Serialization.SerializationException.

Serializability is, as we said, one of .NET's standard attributes, and as such we can discover if an object is serializable using a special mechanism that tells us all the standard attributes defined for a type. The .NET Framework defines an enumeration type named System.Reflection.TypeAttributes, which we can use to determine the standard attributes that were compiled into the type. TypeAttributes yields an integer value, and uses combinations of bits to indicate various pieces of information about a data type. The following table describes some of the 29 enumeration values defined in TypeAttributes ; for a comprehensive list, see TypeAttributes enumeration in Visual Studio .NET Help:

TypeAttributes enumeration	Description
Abstract	Indicates our type is an abstract class, which means we are not allowed to create instances of this class type.
Class	Indicates our type is a class, rather than an interface.
Interface	Indicates our type is an interface.
Serializable	Indicates our type is serializable.

It's also possible to define custom attribute classes of our own, as we'll see later in this chapter. We can use reflection to test for the presence of custom attributes, including predefined custom attributes (such as WebServiceAttribute) and custom attributes that we've written ourselves. To test for custom attributes, call the GetCustomAttribute() or GetCustomAttributes() methods defined in the System.Attribute class and the System.Reflection.MemberInfo class. We'll show how to do this later in the chapter

The following example shows how to test for standard .NET attributes on a data type. We'll show the code listing first, and then discuss the important issues afterwards. You can download the source code for this example from ch05\ ExamineStandardAttributes.vb in the download folder for this book.

```vb
Imports System                      ' For SerializableAttribute class
Imports System.Reflection           ' For TypeAttributes enumeration
Imports System.IO                   ' For file I/O classes
Imports System.Runtime.Serialization.Formatters.Soap   ' SoapFormatter

'  -----------------------------------------------------------------
' This is a serializable class
'  -----------------------------------------------------------------
<Serializable()> _
Public Class MySerializableClass

   Private mData As Integer      ' Some sample data

   Public Sub New(ByVal Data As Integer)
     mData = Data
   End Sub

   Public Overrides Function ToString() As String
     Return "mData is " & mData
   End Function

End Class
```

```vb
' -------------------------------------------------------------------------
' This is not a serializable class
' -------------------------------------------------------------------------
Public Class MyUnserializableClass

  Private mOtherData As String   ' Some sample data

  Public Sub New(ByVal OtherData As String)
    mOtherData = OtherData
  End Sub

  Public Overrides Function ToString() As String
    Return "mOtherData is " & mOtherData
  End Function

End Class

' -------------------------------------------------------------------------
' This is the main class in the application
' -------------------------------------------------------------------------
Public Class MyMainClass

  Public Shared Sub Main()

    MySerialize( New MySerializableClass(42),       "File1.xml" )
    MySerialize( New MySerializableClass(97),       "File2.xml" )
    MySerialize( New MyUnserializableClass("Hello"), "File3.xml" )
    MySerialize( New MyUnserializableClass("World"), "File4.xml" )

  End Sub

  Public Shared Sub MySerialize(ByVal theObject As Object, _
                        ByVal FileName As String)

    ' Get the Type object for the object
    Dim theType As Type = theObject.GetType()

    ' Get the standard attributes defined on this type
    Dim attributes As TypeAttributes = theType.Attributes

    ' Test if this type has the Serializable attribute
    If (attributes And TypeAttributes.Serializable) <> 0 Then

      Console.Write("{0} is a serializable type. ", theType.FullName)

      Dim stream As FileStream = File.Create(FileName)
      Dim formatter As New SoapFormatter()
      formatter.Serialize(stream, theObject)
      stream.Close()
      Console.WriteLine("Serialized object: {0}", theObject)

    Else
```

```
        Console.WriteLine("{0} is NOT a serializable type", _
                        theType.FullName)

    End If

  End Sub

End Class
```

Notice the following points in this sample application:

- ❑ The application defines two classes: `MySerializableClass` is a serializable class, but `MyUnserializableClass` is not.

- ❑ In the `Main()` method in the application, we create some instances of each class, and pass these instances into the `MySerialize()` method.

- ❑ The `MySerialize()` method is declared with an argument type of `Object`, which means it is able to accept any kind of object as an argument. Inside the method, we get the `Type` object associated with this object's type as follows:

```
Dim theType As Type = theObject.GetType()
```

- ❑ The `Type` class has an `Attributes` property, which allows us to get a list of all the attributes defined for our type. The common language runtime inspects our type's metadata, and returns a `TypeAttributes` enumeration value that lists the attributes for our type:

```
Dim attributes As TypeAttributes = theType.Attributes
```

- ❑ We test the attribute list, to see if it includes the `<Serializable()>` attribute. `TypeAttributes` uses bit fields to represent allowable combinations of attributes, so we use a bitwise `And` to test if the `TypeAttributes.Serializable` bits are set:

```
If (attributes And TypeAttributes.Serializable) <> 0 Then
```

Note that `TypeAttributes` is an enumeration value, not a collection. The only way to use a `TypeAttributes` value is to test for explicit attributes, as we have done in the example. It is not possible to iterate through all the attributes that are defined on a type.

- ❑ If the `TypeAttributes.Serializable` bits are set, this indicates our data type is serializable. In this case, we serialize the object to SOAP format as in the earlier example in this chapter. We also use the `FullName` property on the `Type` object, to display the full type name (namespace plus class name) of the object:

```
Console.Write("{0} is a serializable type. ", theType.FullName)

Dim stream As FileStream = File.Create(FileName)
Dim formatter As New SoapFormatter()
formatter.Serialize(stream, theObject)
stream.Close()
Console.WriteLine("Serialized object: {0}", theObject)
```

❏   If the `TypeAttributes.Serializable` bits are not set, this indicates our
    data type is not serializable. If we tried to serialize this object, we'd get a
    `SerializationException`. To avoid this outcome, we display an error
    message on the console instead:

```
Console.WriteLine("{0} is NOT a serializable type", _
                  theType.FullName)
```

When run, the application displays the following messages on the console:

The first two messages on the console indicate the first two objects are serializable. The
final two messages indicate the third and fourth objects are not serializable.

This example has shown how to use the `TypeAttributes` enumeration to test
whether a data type has the `<Serializable()>` attribute. It is also possible to test for
other standard .NET attributes, as illustrated in the following code snippet. This is not
an exhaustive example; for a complete list of standard attributes that you can test, see
TypeAttributes Enumeration in Visual Studio .NET Help.

```
' Is this type an interface?
If (attributes And TypeAttributes.Interface) = _
                 TypeAttributes.Interface Then
  Console.WriteLine("{0} is an interface type", theType.FullName)
End If

' Is this type a public type?
If (attributes And TypeAttributes.Public) = _
                 TypeAttributes.Public Then
  Console.WriteLine("{0} is a public type", theType.FullName)
End If
```

133

```
' Is this type an auto-layout type?
If (attributes And TypeAttributes.AutoLayout) = _
                 TypeAttributes.AutoLayout Then
   Console.WriteLine("{0} is an auto-layout type", theType.FullName)
End If
```

Using Predefined .NET Attributes

In this section, we'll take a detailed look at several predefined attributes in the .NET class library. We'll present a variety of examples that will help you understand attribute syntax, and also give you an appreciation of the wide range of tasks you can achieve using attributes. Here is a list of the examples in this section:

❑   We'll begin by explaining the essential syntax for attribute classes. We'll describe how to determine whether an attribute is applicable for classes, methods, fields, or some other kind of coding element. We'll also describe how to find out whether an attribute requires any mandatory or optional arguments, and show how to provide these arguments.

❑   After we've described the syntactic issues, we'll show how to use the `<Conditional()>` attribute to mark a method as conditionally compiled, depending on whether a preprocessor identifier has been defined.

❑   The final example shows how to define attributes for an entire assembly. We'll show how to specify assembly information such as a title, description, copyright information, and so on.

Understanding Attribute Class Definitions

In order to use attributes effectively, it's essential that you understand the basic syntax of attribute class definitions. You also need to know whether (and how) to pass arguments into an attribute when you use it.

Understanding Attribute Class Syntax

As we mentioned earlier in the chapter, attribute classes inherit from `System.Attribute`, and all the predefined attribute classes in .NET end with the word 'Attribute'. There are two additional restrictions we haven't mentioned yet for attribute classes:

❑   Attribute classes must not be declared as `MustInherit`. In other words, an attribute class must be a concrete class, not an abstract class.

❑   Attribute classes must be preceded by an `<AttributeUsage()>` attribute, which indicates whether the attribute applies to a class, a method, a field, or some other coding element.

We can also use `<AttributeUsage()>` to specify two additional characteristics for an attribute:

❑ We can define whether the attribute can be used multiple times on the same coding element. For example, later in the chapter we'll define an attribute class named `AuthorAttribute`, which we'll use to identify the author of a class. We'll allow `AuthorAttribute` to be used multiple times on the same class, because some classes have multiple authors. We can also define whether the attribute can be inherited by subclasses. For example, we'll indicate that `AuthorAttribute` is not inherited by subclasses, because the author of the subclass might be different than the author of the original class.

To illustrate these rules, let's take a closer look at the `<Serializable()>` attribute we used earlier in the chapter. As you will recall, we can use the `<Serializable()>` attribute to indicate that a class (or structure, enumerated type, or delegate) is serializable. Here is the Visual Studio .NET Help screen for the `<Serializable()>` attribute; to obtain this help screen, type SerializableAttribute class, about SerializableAttribute class in the Visual Studio .NET Help Index field:

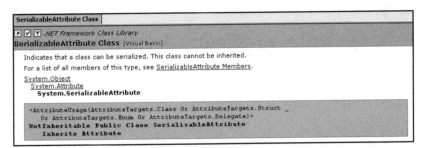

Notice the following points in this screenshot:

❑ The class `SerializableAttribute` is defined in the `System` namespace. Later in the chapter, we'll see many examples of attributes that are defined in different namespaces. In this respect, attribute classes are just like normal classes; they are defined in whichever namespace makes most sense.

❑ `SerializableAttribute` inherits from `System.Attribute`. All attribute classes inherit from `System.Attribute`.

❑ `SerializableAttribute` is not declared as `MustInherit`, which means it is a concrete class. However, notice that `SerializableAttribute` is declared as `NotInheritable`, which means it is a sealed class; we cannot derive new subclasses from `SerializableAttribute`. This is a particular facet of the `SerializableAttribute` class; there is no intrinsic .NET requirement for attribute classes to be declared as `NotInheritable`.

The fact that SerializableAttribute *is* NotInheritable *indicates that this attribute class has not been designed for extension through inheritance. The designers and authors of* SerializableAttribute *at Microsoft have decided that this class is already complete, and there are no situations where a specialized subclass might be necessary.*

❑   The SerializableAttribute class definition is preceded by an <AttributeUsage()> attribute, which specifies where and how the <Serializable()> attribute can be used. The <AttributeUsage()> attribute for <Serializable()> is defined as follows:

```
<AttributeUsage(AttributeTargets.Class Or AttributeTargets.Struct _
    Or AttributeTargets.Enum Or AttributeTargets.Delegate)>
```

This indicates that the <Serializable()> attribute can be applied to class types, structures types, enumeration types, and delegate types. In other words, it is possible to serialize class objects, structure objects, enumeration objects, and delegate objects.

<AttributeUsage()> uses an enumeration type named AttributeTargets to specify the allowable targets for an attribute. For example, AttributeTargets.Class indicates an attribute can be applied to class definitions, AttributeTargets.Struct indicates an attribute can be applied to structure definitions, and so on. The following table shows a complete list of AttributeTargets values; these can be bitwise-Or'd together, as shown in the above example, to specify multiple target types:

AttributeTargets enumeration	Description and example
AttributeTargets.All	The attribute in question can be applied to any coding element. An example of an attribute with this usage is <CLSCompliant()>, which indicates a coding element complies with the rules defined in the .NET common language specification.
AttributeTargets.Assembly	The attribute in question can be applied to an assembly. An example of an attribute with this usage is <AssemblyVersion()>, which specifies the version number for an assembly.

AttributeTargets enumeration	Description and example
AttributeTargets.Class	The attribute in question can be applied to a class.
	An example of an attribute with this usage is `<WebService()>`, which specifies information about web service classes.
AttributeTargets.Constructor	The attribute in question can be applied to a constructor.
	An example of an attribute with this usage is `<FileIOPermission()>`. We can annotate constructors with this attribute, to indicate that the code in the constructor uses declarative security checks when accessing files in the file system.
	You can also use `<FileIOPermission()>` on assemblies, classes, structures, and methods.
AttributeTargets.Delegate	The attribute in question can be applied to a delegate.
	An example of an attribute with this usage is `<ComVisible()>`, which specifies whether a .NET delegate should be made visible to COM when you export a .NET component to COM clients.
	You can also use `<ComVisible()>` to specify COM visibility for .NET assemblies, classes, structures, enums, fields, methods, properties, and interfaces.
AttributeTargets.Enum	The attribute in question can be applied to an enumeration.
	An example of an attribute with this usage is `<Obsolete()>`, which specifies that an enumeration is obsolete.
	You can also use `<Obsolete()>` to mark classes, structures, interfaces, constructors, methods, properties, fields, events, and delegates as obsolete.

Table continued on following page

AttributeTargets enumeration	Description and example
AttributeTargets.Event	The attribute in question can be applied to an event.
	An example of an attribute with this usage is `<DispId()>`, which specifies the COM DispId of an event.
	You can also use `<DispId()>` to specify the COM DispId of methods, properties, and fields.
AttributeTargets.Field	The attribute in question can be applied to a field.
	An example of an attribute with this usage is `<NonSerialized()>`, which indicates that a particular field in a serializable class should not be serialized.
AttributeTargets.Interface	The attribute in question can be applied to an interface.
	An example of an attribute with this usage is `<InterfaceType()>`, which we can use when we export a .NET interface to COM. The attribute indicates whether the interface should be exposed as a dual interface, an IDispatch-based interface, or an IUnknown-based interface.
AttributeTargets.Method	The attribute in question can be applied to a method.
	An example of an attribute with this usage is `<WebMethod()>`, which indicates that a method is a web service method.
AttributeTargets.Module	The attribute in question can be applied to a module (that is, a DLL or EXE file that comprises a multi-file assembly).
	An example of an attribute with this usage is `<Debuggable()>`, which indicates that a module supports just-in-time debugging.
	You can also use `<Debuggable()>` on assemblies.

AttributeTargets enumeration	Description and example
AttributeTargets.Parameter	The attribute in question can be applied to a parameter.
	An example of an attribute with this usage is `<ParamArray()>`, which specifies that a method allows a variable number of parameters to be passed in. The parameters will be delivered to the method as an array.
AttributeTargets.Property	The attribute in question can be applied to a property.
	An example of an attribute with this usage is `<IndexerName()>`, which specifies the name of the indexer method in a class, for the benefit of programming languages that do not directly provide special syntax for indexers.
AttributeTargets.ReturnValue	The attribute in question can be applied to a return value from a method or property.
	An example of an attribute with this usage is `<XmlElement()>`. This attribute can be used (amongst other reasons) to specify the allowable types of elements in an array, when a method returns an array of objects. This information is required by the XML serializer, so that it knows what data types to expect in the returned array.
AttributeTargets.Struct	The attribute in question can be applied to a structure.
	An example of an attribute with this usage is `<StructLayout()>`, which specifies a particular layout for fields in a structure. This is important when you pass structures to unmanaged APIs, because the unmanaged API usually expects a particular layout for fields in the structure.
	You can also use `<StructLayout()>` on classes.

Passing Arguments into Attributes

Another important characteristic of attributes is whether they require any arguments. The `<Serializable()>` attribute is a fairly simple example, because it doesn't require any arguments at all; when we use `<Serializable()>` to mark a class as serializable, we don't need to pass any extra information in the attribute's parentheses:

```
<Serializable()> _      ' No need to pass any arguments between the ()
Public Class Account
   ' Members...
End Class
```

However, many attributes do require arguments in order to provide supporting information for the attribute. There are two kinds of arguments for attributes:

❑ Positional arguments. These arguments are mandatory, and must be supplied in a specific order at the beginning of the attribute's argument list. Positional arguments are passed into the attribute's constructor, to perform essential initialization for the attribute. To find out what positional arguments are required for an attribute, consult the documentation for the attribute's constructor(s).

The following example illustrates positional arguments. The example shows how to use `<DllImport()>` to expose the `MessageBeep()` Win32 API to a .NET application. The `DllImportAttribute` constructor takes a single `String` parameter, which indicates the name of the DLL that contains the Win32 API. The `MessageBeep()` API resides in `User32.dll`, so we specify the parameter `"User32.dll"` in the `<DllImport()>` attribute:

```
<DllImport("User32.dll")> _
Public Shared Function MessageBeep(type As Integer) As Boolean
   ' Leave function empty: this is just a wrapper for the Win32 API
End Function
```

❑ Named arguments. These arguments are optional, and can be supplied in any order after the positional arguments in the attribute's argument list. Named arguments correspond to the names of fields or properties in the attribute class. You must use `:=` syntax to assign a value to a named argument.

The following example illustrates named arguments. The example shows how to use `<DllImport()>` to expose the `MessageBox()` Win32 API to .NET. The `DllImportAttribute` class has properties named `CharSet` and `EntryPoint` (amongst others), which allow us to provide supplemental information about the API we want to expose:

```
<DllImport("User32.dll", _
           CharSet := CharSet.Unicode, _
           EntryPoint := "MessageBoxW")> _
```

```
Public Shared Function MessageBox(hWnd As IntPtr, _
                                  text As String, _
                                  caption As String, _
                                  type As Integer) As Integer
   ' Leave function empty: this is just a wrapper for the Win32 API
End Function
```

For more information about the `<DllImport()>` attribute and the
`MessageBox()` Win32 API, see Visual Studio .NET Help.

To further illustrate the rules for positional and named arguments in an attribute, we'll consider the `TransactionAttribute` class defined in the `System.EnterpriseServices` namespace. `TransactionAttribute` allows us to specify automatic transactional support for a .NET class, and enables us to write .NET code that integrates easily with COM+ transactions and database transactions.

We won't go into the details of transactions in .NET here. For more
information, see Professional VB.NET Transactions, ISBN 1-86100-595-4,
published by Wrox Press.

The `TransactionAttribute` class has two constructors, with the following signatures:

```
' No-arg constructor for the TransactionAttribute class,
' which sets the automatic transaction type to "required".
Public Sub New()

' One-arg constructor for the TransactionAttribute class, which allows
' us to choose the level of automatic transaction support we need.
Public Sub New(ByVal Val As TransactionOption)
```

The following code snippet shows how to use the first constructor in a `<Transaction()>` attribute. The compiler calls the `TransactionAttribute` no-argument constructor, which sets the transaction type to "required" for `MyClass1`:

```
<Transaction()> _
Public Class MyClass1
   ' Members...
End Class
```

The next code snippet shows how to use the parameterized constructor in a `<Transaction()>` attribute. The compiler calls the second `TransactionAttribute` constructor listed above, and passes `TransactionOption.RequiresNew` as a parameter. This sets the transaction type to "requires new" for `MyClass2`, which means the runtime is obliged to create a new transaction whenever a `MyClass2` object is created:

141

```
<Transaction(TransactionOption.RequiresNew)> _
Public Class MyClass2
  ' Members...
End Class
```

In addition to the constructors defined in the `TransactionAttribute` class, there are also two public get/set properties as follows:

```
' Get or set the transaction isolation level
Public Property Isolation As TransactionIsolationLevel
  Get
    ' Get the isolation level defined by this TransactionAttribute
  End Get
  Set(ByVal Value As TransactionIsolationLevel)
    ' Set the isolation level for this TransactionAttribute
  End Set
End Property

' Get or set the transaction timeout value
Public Property Timeout As Integer
  Get
    ' Get the timeout defined by this TransactionAttribute
  End Get
  Set(ByVal Value As Integer)
    ' Set the timeout for this TransactionAttribute
  End Set
End Property
```

We can use these properties to provide optional additional initialization when we use the `<Transaction()>` attribute.

The following example shows how to use these properties in conjunction with the no-argument constructor for `TransactionAttribute`. In this example, we indicate that `MyClass3` has the "repeatable read" isolation level, which means that data in a database is locked during a SQL query operation. The transaction time-out is set to 10 seconds, which means each transactional operation must complete in this timespan:

```
<Transaction(Isolation := TransactionIsolationLevel.RepeatableRead, _
             Timeout := 10)> _
Public Class MyClass3
  ' Members...
End Class
```

The order of property assignments is insignificant, providing the property assignments come after any constructor arguments. The following example shows how to combine constructor arguments and optional property assignments in an attribute declaration. The constructor argument comes first, followed by the property assignments; note that constructor arguments do not have a name as such, so we do not use the syntax name := value for constructor arguments:

```
<Transaction(TransactionOption.RequiresNew,    _
             Isolation := TransactionIsolationLevel.RepeatableRead, _
             Timeout := 10)> _
Public Class MyClass4
  ' Members...
End Class
```

That concludes our survey of attribute syntax. We've described the meaning of the syntax in attribute class definitions, and seen how to pass mandatory and optional arguments into attribute declarations. Equipped with this knowledge, we shall now embark on a series of examples that will give you a flavor of the diverse use of attributes in .NET. Once we've done that, we'll see how to define and use new custom attribute classes of our own.

Hold on tight, we're going in...

Using Attributes to Control the Compiler

In this example, we'll see how to use the <Conditional()> attribute to mark a method as conditionally compiled. Calls to the method will only be compiled if a specified preprocessor identifier is defined; if the identifier is not defined, the Visual Basic .NET compiler will ignore calls to the method in our code. By using the <Conditional()> attribute, we don't need to comment out our diagnostic code for a release version of the application. Thus attributes enable us to give 'context' to our code; which is very convenient and a major boost to developer efficiency, particularly when we have a very large and complex application that may span many versions and had a multitude of developers working on it.

The following application shows a typical use of the <Conditional()> attribute, to display diagnostic information about the current state of an object. You can download the source code for this example from ch05\ ConditionalCompilation.vb in the download folder for this book.

In this example, we define an Account class that represents a simple bank account; the class keeps track of the current balance, and uses an ArrayList to record every deposit and withdrawal. The Deposit() and Withdraw() methods call a diagnostic method named MyDumpStatus(), to display the current state of the Account object before performing deposit or withdrawal operations. This information will help us verify that the Account object is in a valid state before the operation takes place. The MyDumpStatus() method is annotated with the <Conditional("Debug")> attribute, which means method invocations will only be compiled if the Debug preprocessor identifier is defined:

```
Imports System              ' For Console and String classes
Imports System.Collections  ' For ArrayList class
Imports System.Diagnostics  ' For Conditional attribute
```

```vb
Public Class Account

  ' Fields
  Private mName As String
  Private mBalance As Double
  Private mActivity As ArrayList

  ' Constructor
  Public Sub New(ByVal Name As String)
    mName = Name
    mBalance = 0.0
    mActivity = new ArrayList()
  End Sub

  ' Deposit funds
  Public Sub Deposit(ByVal Amount As Double)
    MyDumpStatus( String.Format("About to deposit {0:C}", Amount) )
    mBalance += Amount
    mActivity.Add(Amount)
  End Sub

  ' Withdraw funds
  Public Sub Withdraw(ByVal Amount As Double)
    MyDumpStatus( String.Format("About to withdraw {0:C}", Amount) )
    mBalance -= Amount
    mActivity.Add(-Amount)
  End Sub

  ' Return object's state as a string
  Public Overrides Function ToString() As String
    Return String.Format("{0}, {1:C}", mName, mBalance)
  End Function

  ' Calls to this method will only be compiled if "Debug" is defined
  <Conditional("Debug")> _
  Public Sub MyDumpStatus(ByVal Message As String)

    Console.WriteLine("-------------------------------------------")
    Console.WriteLine("MyDump STATUS: {0}", Message)
    Console.WriteLine("-------------------------------------------")

    Console.WriteLine("Name {0}, balance {1:C}", mName, mBalance)
    Dim index As Integer
    For index = 0 To mActivity.Count - 1
      Console.WriteLine("  ({0})  {1:C}", index, mActivity(index))
    Next
    Console.WriteLine()

  End Sub

End Class
```

```
' This is the main class in the application, to test the Account class
Public Class MainClass
  Public Shared Sub Main()
    Dim acc1 As New Account("Joseph")
    acc1.Deposit(1000)
    acc1.Deposit(5000)
    acc1.Withdraw(2000)
    acc1.Deposit(3000)
    Console.WriteLine("FINAL STATUS: {0}", acc1)
  End Sub
End Class
```

To take control of the preprocessor symbols, we'll use the command line compiler. Let's see what happens if we compile the application as follows, without defining the Debug preprocessor symbol:

> **vbc ConditionalCompilation.vb**

To run the application, type the following command:

> **ConditionalCompilation.exe**

The application displays the following message on the console:

As you can see, there is no diagnostic information here. Let's take a look at the MSIL for the application, to see what's happening. Type the following command to run the MSIL Disassembler:

> **ildasm.exe ConditionalCompilation.exe**

When the MSIL Disassembler window appears, double-click the MyDumpStatus() method of the Account class. The MSIL code for this method is displayed as follows:

```
.method public instance void  MyDumpStatus(string Message) cil managed
{
  .custom instance void
    [mscorlib]System.Diagnostics.ConditionalAttribute::.ctor(string) =
              ( 01 00 05 44 65 62 75 67 00 00 )       // ...Debug..
```

145

```
      // Additional implementation code for MyDumpStatus() not shown...

   }
```

The first MSIL statement inside the method is a call to the constructor for the
ConditionalAttribute class, passing the string "Debug" as an argument. This indicates
the method is conditionally compiled, depending on whether the Debug preprocessor
identifier is defined. We'll see how to define this preprocessor identifier shortly.

Close this window, and return to the main MSIL Disassembler window. Now double-
click the Deposit() method, to see the MSIL code for this method:

```
.method public instance void  Deposit(float64 Amount) cil managed
{
  // Code size       33 (0x21)
  .maxstack  8
  IL_0000:  ldarg.0
  IL_0001:  ldarg.0
  IL_0002:  ldfld      float64 Account::mBalance
  IL_0007:  ldarg.1
  IL_0008:  add
  IL_0009:  stfld      float64 Account::mBalance
  IL_000e:  ldarg.0
  IL_000f:  ldfld      class [mscorlib]System.Collections.ArrayList
                       Account::mActivity
  IL_0014:  ldarg.1
  IL_0015:  box        [mscorlib]System.Double
  IL_001a:  callvirt   instance int32 [mscorlib]
                       System.Collections.ArrayList::Add(object)
  IL_001f:  pop
  IL_0020:  ret
} // end of method Account::Deposit
```

Notice that the Deposit() method does not contain any instructions to call the
MyDumpStatus() method, because the Debug preprocessor identifier isn't defined.

If we want diagnostic information to be displayed, we must recompile our application
with the Debug preprocessor identifier defined as follows:

> **vbc   -d:Debug=1 ConditionalCompilation.vb**

When we run the application, it now displays diagnostic information on the console:

Here is the revised MSIL for the Deposit() method, now that the Debug preprocessor identifier has been defined. Notice that the statements numbered IL_0001 through to IL_0011 call the MyDumpStatus() method with an appropriately-formatted diagnostic message:

```
.method public instance void  Deposit(float64 Amount) cil managed
{
  // Code size       55 (0x37)
  .maxstack  8
  IL_0000:  ldarg.0
  IL_0001:  ldstr       "About to deposit {0:C}"
  IL_0006:  ldarg.1
  IL_0007:  box         [mscorlib]System.Double
  IL_000c:  call        string [mscorlib]System.String::Format(string,
                                                               object)
  IL_0011:  callvirt    instance void Account::MyDumpStatus(string)
  IL_0016:  ldarg.0
  IL_0017:  ldarg.0
  IL_0018:  ldfld       float64 Account::mBalance
  IL_001d:  ldarg.1
  IL_001e:  add
  IL_001f:  stfld       float64 Account::mBalance
  IL_0024:  ldarg.0
```

```
IL_0025:  ldfld       class [mscorlib]System.Collections.ArrayList
                      Account::mActivity
IL_002a:  ldarg.1
IL_002b:  box         [mscorlib]System.Double
IL_0030:  callvirt    instance int32 [mscorlib]
                      System.Collections.ArrayList::Add(object)
IL_0035:  pop
IL_0036:  ret
} // end of method Account::Deposit
```

One final point: the MSIL code for the `MyDumpStatus()` method is the same as before. The `<Conditional()>` attribute determines whether the compiler should compile calls to the method; the method itself is always compiled into the same MSIL.

Defining and Using Assembly Attributes

When we create a Visual Basic .NET project in Visual Studio .NET, the project automatically contains a file named `AssemblyInfo.vb`. This file contains global attributes such as `<AssemblyTitle()>` and `<AssemblyDescription()>`, which provide metadata for the assembly as a whole.

Global attributes must be defined directly after any `Imports` statements, and outside of any namespace or type definitions. The reason for this latter restriction is because assemblies can comprise multiple namespaces; in order for global attributes to apply across all these namespaces, the attributes must be defined outside of any namespace definition.

The general syntax for declaring assembly attributes is as follows. `Assembly` is a Visual Basic .NET keyword, and indicates that the attribute applies to the entire assembly:

```
<Assembly: AttributeDeclaration>
```

It is also possible to declare global attributes for a specific module in an assembly. The general syntax for declaring module attributes is as follows. `Module` is a Visual Basic .NET keyword, and indicates (in this context) that the attribute applies just to the current .NET module:

```
<Module: AttributeDeclaration>
```

To illustrate how to define and use assembly attributes, we have provided a sample Visual Basic .NET project named `AssemblyAttributeDemo.sln`, which you can find in the download code folder `ch05\AssemblyAttributeDemo`.

The `AssemblyInfo.vb` source file contains a variety of assembly attributes, as follows. These attributes are fairly self explanatory, but we've written some comments nonetheless:

```
Imports System.Reflection              ' For Assembly attributes
Imports System.Runtime.InteropServices ' For GuidAttribute

' User-friendly title for this assembly
<Assembly: AssemblyTitle("Greetings assembly")>

' Additional descriptive text for this assembly
<Assembly: AssemblyDescription("This assembly displays a time-
sensitive greeting")>

' Name of the company that developed the assembly
<Assembly: AssemblyCompany("My Cool Company Ltd")>

' Product name
<Assembly: AssemblyProduct("My Cool Product")>

' Copyright information
<Assembly: AssemblyCopyright("© Copyright My Cool Company, 2002")>

' Trademark information
<Assembly: AssemblyTrademark("TM My Cool Company Ltd")>

' This assembly is CLS-compliant
<Assembly: CLSCompliant(True)>

'The following GUID is for the ID of the typelib if this project
' is exposed to COM (this GUID was generated by Visual Studio .NET)
<Assembly: Guid("DABB3C50-F150-4743-977A-C670902EC183")>

' Version information for an assembly consists of four values:
'    Major Version : Minor Version : Build Number : Revision
<Assembly: AssemblyVersion("1.0.*")>
```

In a moment, we'll build the application and see how to view the assembly's metadata. Before we do that, we'll introduce a new technique for inspecting custom attributes programmatically. Here is the high-level code in the MainClass.vb source file:

```
Imports System               ' For miscellaneous classes
Imports System.Reflection    ' For Attribute class

Public Class MainClass

  ' This is the entry point of the application
  Public Shared Sub Main()
    DisplayGreeting()
    DisplayAssemblyTitle()
    DisplayAssemblyDescription()
  End Sub

  Public Shared Sub DisplayGreeting()
    ' See below...
  End Sub
```

149

```
      Public Shared Sub DisplayAssemblyTitle()
         ' See below...
      End Sub

      Public Shared Sub DisplayAssemblyDescription()
         ' See below...
      End Sub

   End Class
```

The `DisplayGreeting()` method isn't directly relevant to the reflection code, but it adds a little more personality to the application's startup:

```
Public Shared Sub DisplayGreeting()
   Dim currentHour As Integer = DateTime.Now.Hour
   If currentHour < 12 Then
      Console.WriteLine("Good morning!")
   ElseIf currentHour < 18 Then
      Console.WriteLine("Good afternoon!")
   Else
      Console.WriteLine("Good evening!")
   End If
End Sub
```

The `DisplayAssemblyTitle()` method shown below illustrates how to test for custom attributes programmatically. Study the code first, and then read the explanations that follow.

```
Public Shared Sub DisplayAssemblyTitle()

   ' Get the custom attribute, AssemblyTitleAttribute
   Dim attr As Attribute
   attr = Attribute.GetCustomAttribute( _
                     [Assembly].GetCallingAssembly(), _
                     GetType(AssemblyTitleAttribute), _
                     False)

   ' Convert attr to actual data type, AssemblyTitleAttribute
   Dim ta As AssemblyTitleAttribute
   ta = CType(attr, AssemblyTitleAttribute)

   ' Display the AssemblyTitleAttribute's Title property
   If Not (ta Is Nothing) Then
      Console.WriteLine("AssemblyTitle attribute: {0}", ta.Title)
   Else
      Console.WriteLine("AssemblyTitle attribute not found")
   End If

End Sub
```

Note the following points in the `DisplayAssemblyTitle()` method shown above:

❏ The `Attribute.GetCustomAttribute()` method allows us to retrieve a specific attribute on a particular coding element (such as an assembly, a class, a method, and so on). `Attribute` is a standard .NET class that enables us to perform attribute-related programming tasks in our code.

In this example, we use `GetCustomAttribute()` method to get the `<AssemblyTitle()>` attribute for the current assembly. Note that `Assembly` is both a class name and a keyword in Visual Basic .NET, so we must use the escape syntax `[Assembly]` to indicate we're using the `Assembly` class name rather than the `Assembly` keyword:

```
Dim attr As Attribute
attr = Attribute.GetCustomAttribute( _
                 [Assembly].GetCallingAssembly(), _
                 GetType(AssemblyTitleAttribute), _
                 False)
```

❏ The `GetCustomAttribute()` method can be used to retrieve any kind of custom attribute, and consequently the method has a declared return type of `Attribute`. We therefore use `CType` to convert the retrieved attribute into the correct data type, namely `AssemblyTitleAttribute`.

```
Dim ta As AssemblyTitleAttribute
ta = CType(attr, AssemblyTitleAttribute)
```

❏ The `AssemblyTitleAttribute` has a `Title` property, which indicates the title of the assembly. We display this information on the console window as follows (the `If` test guards against the possibility that our assembly doesn't have an `AssemblyTitleAttribute`):

```
If Not (ta Is Nothing) Then
   Console.WriteLine("AssemblyTitle attribute: {0}", ta.Title)
Else
   Console.WriteLine("AssemblyTitle attribute not found")
End If
```

Now let's see how to implement the `DisplayAssemblyDescription()` method, to display the `<AssemblyDescription()>` custom attribute. This method is essentially the same as `DisplayAssemblyTitle`, except that it retrieves `AssemblyDescriptionAttribute` rather than `AssemblyTitleAttribute`. The only other difference is that `AssemblyDescriptionAttribute` has a `Description` property, whereas `AssemblyTitleAttribute` has a `Title` property:

```
Public Shared Sub DisplayAssemblyDescription()

    ' Get the custom attribute, AssemblyDescriptionAttribute
    Dim attr As Attribute
    attr = Attribute.GetCustomAttribute( _
                        [Assembly].GetCallingAssembly(), _
                        GetType(AssemblyDescriptionAttribute), _
                        False)

    ' Convert attr to actual data type, AssemblyDescriptionAttribute
    Dim da As AssemblyDescriptionAttribute
    da = CType(attr, AssemblyDescriptionAttribute)

    ' Display the AssemblyDescriptionAttribute's Description property
    If Not (da Is Nothing) Then
        Console.WriteLine("AssemblyDescription: {0}", da.Description)
    Else
        Console.WriteLine("AssemblyDescription attribute not found")
    End If

End Sub
```

When we build and run the application, it displays the following information on the console. Notice the assembly title and assembly description are displayed as expected:

It's also possible to view the assembly metadata using Windows Explorer. Navigate to the folder that contains the assembly file AssemblyAttributeDemo.exe, and view the properties for the file. The Properties window appears as follows; notice that the assembly's description corresponds to the <AssemblyTitle()>attribute we specified earlier:

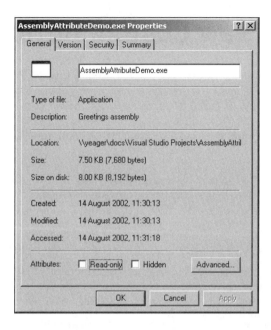

To obtain more detailed information, click the Version tab at the top of the Properties window. This allows us to inspect any aspect of assembly metadata, simply by selecting one of the entries in the Item name list box on the left-hand side of the window:

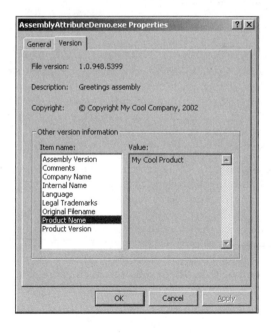

Defining New Custom Attributes

This is the final section of the chapter. In this section, we'll see how to define new custom attribute classes, and how to use these attributes on a variety of coding elements such as classes and methods. We'll also recap how to access custom attributes on a coding element, by using the `Attribute.GetCustomAttribute()` method.

Defining a custom attribute class isn't that much different from defining a normal class. Here's a reminder of the distinguishing features of attribute classes:

❑ Attribute classes must be preceded by an `<AttributeUsage()>` attribute, to specify the applicability of the attribute class. The `<AttributeUsage()>` attribute can specify three pieces of information:

  • The allowable kinds of target for the attribute, such as a class, a structure, a field, and so on. This information is mandatory.

  • Whether the attribute can be applied multiple times on the same code element. Specify `AllowMultiple:=True` or `AllowMultiple:=False`; the default is `False`.

  • Whether the attribute is inherited by subclasses. Specify `Inherited:=True` or `Inherited:=False`; the default is `True`.

❑ Attribute classes must inherit (directly or indirectly) from `System.Attribute`.

❑ Attribute classes cannot be declared as `MustInherit`.

❑ By convention, attribute classes should end with the word `'Attribute'`.

❑ Attribute classes should define constructor(s) to receive mandatory initialization parameters. Developers are forced to supply these parameters in the order they appear in the constructor(s). If we want to allow the developer a bit more flexibility, we can define a variety of constructors each taking different combinations of arguments; the developer can choose which constructor to specify when they use the attribute.

❑ Attribute classes may define get/set properties to receive optional initialization parameters. Developers can supply these parameters in any order, after the constructor parameters.

There are strict limitations on the parameters that a programmer using your attributes will be able to pass in to your attribute. The only expressions which are valid in an attribute declaration are called constant expressions; that is, they must be able to be wholly evaluated at compile-time. The result of such an expression must belong to one of the following types:

- ❏ Byte
- ❏ Short
- ❏ Integer
- ❏ Long
- ❏ Char
- ❏ Single
- ❏ Double
- ❏ Decimal
- ❏ Boolean
- ❏ String
- ❏ any enumeration type
- ❏ the null type

The coder using your attribute will be able to specify expressions involving literals, references to constants defined in other types, and specific enumeration values, but won't be able to call methods or VB.NET functions, or access reference types.

The following example illustrates these rules for defining attribute classes. You can download the source code for this example from ch05\MyCustomAttributes.vb in the download folder for this book.

We'll begin with the Imports statements:

```
Imports System            ' For miscellaneous classes
Imports System.Reflection    ' For Attribute class
```

Next, let's define a custom attribute class named AuthorAttribute. This attribute will contain information about the author of a class, structure, or interface. Multiple <Author()> attributes are allowed on the same target, but <Author()> attributes are not inherited by subclasses. Furthermore, when a programmer uses an <Author()> attribute on their class, structure, or interface, they must specify the author's name as a parameter to the <Author()> attribute.

```
<AttributeUsage(AttributeTargets.Class  Or  _
                AttributeTargets.Struct Or  _
                AttributeTargets.Interface, _
                AllowMultiple := True,  _
                Inherited := False)> _
Public Class AuthorAttribute
   Inherits Attribute

   Private mAuthor As String
```

```
   Public Sub New(ByVal Author As String)
      mAuthor = Author
   End Sub

   Public ReadOnly Property Author As String
      Get
         Return mAuthor
      End Get
   End Property

   Public Overrides Function ToString() As String
      Return "Author: " & mAuthor
   End Function

End Class
```

Now let's define another custom attribute class named ModifiedAttribute. This attribute will contain information about when a class, structure, or interface was modified by a programmer. This is the sort of information you typically find in a version control system. Multiple <Modified()> attributes are allowed on the same target, but <Modified()> attributes are not inherited by subclasses. When a programmer uses a <Modified()> attribute on their class, structure, or interface, they must provide their name and a severity number (for example, 1=severe bug, 2=important bug, and so on). Optionally, the programmer can also provide a textual description of the modification they made to the class, structure, or interface:

```
   <AttributeUsage(AttributeTargets.Class  Or  _
                   AttributeTargets.Struct Or  _
                   AttributeTargets.Interface, _
                   AllowMultiple := True,  _
                   Inherited := False)> _
Public Class ModifiedAttribute
   Inherits Attribute

   Private mWho As String
   Private mSeverity As Integer
   Private mDescription As String

   Public Sub New(ByVal Who As String, ByVal Severity As Integer)
      mWho = Who
      mSeverity = Severity
   End Sub

   Public ReadOnly Property Who As String
      Get
         Return mWho
      End Get
   End Property
```

```
Public ReadOnly Property Severity As Integer
   Get
      Return mSeverity
   End Get
End Property

Public Property Description As String
   Get
      If mDescription Is Nothing Then
         Return "(no description)"
      Else
         Return mDescription
      End If
   End Get
   Set
      mDescription = Value
   End Set
End Property

Public Overrides Function ToString() As String
   Return "Modified by: "   & Who & _
          ", severity: "    & Severity & _
          ", description: " & Description
End Function

End Class
```

Now let's see how to use the custom attributes, <Author()> and <Modified()>, in our classes, structures, and interfaces. The following example shows how to use these attributes. You can download the source code for this example from ch05\UseCustomAttributes.vb in the download folder for this book.

As before, we'll begin with the Imports statements:

```
Imports System             ' For miscellaneous classes
Imports System.Reflection  ' For Attribute class
```

The following interface shows how to define a single <Author()> attribute:

```
<Author("Jayne")> _
Public Interface IBookable

   ' Members...

End Interface
```

The following class shows how to define multiple <Author()> attributes on the same target:

157

```
<Author("Thomas"), _
 Author("Emily")> _
Public Class Hotel
  Implements IBookable

    ' Members...

End Class
```

The following class shows how to define multiple `<Author()>` and `<Modified()>` attributes on the same target. Notice that the first `<Modified()>` attribute provides an optional `Description`, but the second `<Modified()>` attribute does not provide a `Description`:

```
<Author("Andy"), _
 Modified("Nigel",  3, Description:="Fixed Andy's bugs!"), _
 Modified("Simon",  4)> _
Public Structure SkiLift

    Private mCapacityPerHour As Integer

End Structure
```

We can use reflection to retrieve the set of custom attributes on a particular coding element. The following code shows what we need to do. In this example, the `MyDisplayAttributes()` method receives a `MemberInfo` parameter containing reflection information for a coding element. We call `MyDisplayAttributes()` three times, passing in `Type` objects representing the `IBookable`, `Hotel`, and `SkiLift` types (note that `Type` is derived from `MemberInfo`, so there is no problem passing `Type` parameters into the `MyDisplayAttributes()` method).

`MemberInfo` has a `GetCustomAttributes()` method, which returns an array of custom attributes defined on the coding element (the `False` parameter in the `GetCustomAttributes()` method means we aren't interested in any custom attributes defined in our superclass). In this example, we simply use a loop to display the information contained in each custom attribute:

```
Public Class MainClass

  Public Shared Sub Main()
    MyDisplayAttributes( GetType(IBookable) )
    MyDisplayAttributes( GetType(Hotel) )
    MyDisplayAttributes( GetType(SkiLift) )
  End Sub

  Public Shared Sub MyDisplayAttributes(ByVal info As MemberInfo)

    Console.WriteLine("-----------------------------------------------")
    Console.WriteLine("Custom attributes for type {0}", info)
    Console.WriteLine("-----------------------------------------------")
```

```
    Dim attribs As Object() = info.GetCustomAttributes(False)
    Dim i As Integer
    For i = 0 To attribs.Length - 1
      Console.WriteLine("{0}", attribs(i))
    Next i
    Console.WriteLine()

  End Sub

End Class
```

The application displays the following information on the console. If you run this application yourself, you may find the attributes are displayed in a different order; the ordering of attributes retrieved by GetCustomAttributes() is not guaranteed:

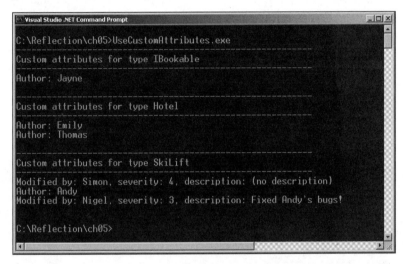

This example shows how to define custom attributes with a combination of mandatory and optional parameters, and how to use these custom attributes when we define new data types. The example also shows how to use reflection to retrieve the custom attributes programmatically.

This opens the door to an entirely new style of programming in .NET. Here are some examples of the kinds of tasks we can achieve using custom attributes:

❑ Define a visual appearance for fields and properties defined in a class. Create an attribute class that specifies the font name, color, and other visual features for each field and property.

❑ Map classes and structures to tables in a relational database. Create an attribute class that specifies the name of the database that contains data, which can be used to initialize instances of the class or structure. Map fields and properties to columns in a database table. Create an attribute class that identifies the name of the appropriate column for a specific field of property.

159

These are just a few suggestions for using custom attributes. We're sure you can think of many more!

The attributes we've explored here all only spring into action when they are examined reflectively by other code. However, there is a class in the .NET framework, `System.ContextBoundObject`, part of the .NET remoting infrastructure, which automatically activates any attributes that extend `System.Runtime.Remoting.Contexts.ContextAttribute` associated with it. It is possible, using this class as a base for our own classes, to create attributes that are activated whenever the class is instantiated, or its methods are called. Unfortunately, much of the required functionality to do so is undocumented in the current release of .NET, since it is only really used internally by .NET itself. As a quick demonstration of what's seemingly possible with context-bound attributes, we can put together a simple method-call logging framework.

Take a look at the following code – most of which is just boilerplate for a context-bound attribute:

```vb
Imports System
Imports System.Runtime.Remoting.Contexts
Imports System.Runtime.Remoting.Messaging
Imports System.Runtime.Remoting.Activation

Public Class LoggedAttribute
  Inherits ContextAttribute
  Implements IContributeObjectSink, IMessageSink

  Private _nextSink As IMessageSink
  Private _target As MarshalByRefObject

  Public Sub New()
    MyBase.New("Logging Service")
  End Sub

  Public Overrides Sub GetPropertiesForNewContext _
                      (ByVal ccm As IConstructionCallMessage)
    ccm.ContextProperties.Add(Me)
  End Sub

  Public Function GetObjectSink(ByVal target As MarshalByRefObject, _
                ByVal nextSink As IMessageSink) As IMessageSink _
        Implements IContributeObjectSink.GetObjectSink
    _target = target
    _nextSink = nextSink
    Return Me
  End Function

  Public ReadOnly Property NextSink() As IMessageSink _
        Implements IMessageSink.NextSink
    Get
```

```
         Return _nextSink
      End Get
   End Property

   Public ReadOnly Property Target() As MarshalByRefObject
      Get
         Return _target
      End Get
   End Property
```

After the basic lifecycle methods are out of the way, we can get on with handling messages inbound to the object to which we're attached. We have to handle synchronous and asynchronous messages. In both cases, we pass the object representing the inbound message to another procedure for handling:

```
   Public Function SyncProcessMessage(ByVal msg As IMessage) _
            As IMessage Implements IMessageSink.SyncProcessMessage
      HandleCall(msg)
      Return _nextSink.SyncProcessMessage(msg)
   End Function

   Public Function AsyncProcessMessage(ByVal msg As IMessage, _
            ByVal replySink As IMessageSink) As IMessageCtrl _
         Implements IMessageSink.AsyncProcessMessage
      HandleCall(msg)
      Return _nextSink.AsyncProcessMessage(msg, replySink)
   End Function
```

Now, we extract the name of the called method, and display a message box:

```
   Private Sub HandleCall(ByVal msg As IMessage)
      Dim name As String = msg.Properties("__MethodName")
      If Not name Is Nothing Then
         MsgBox(String.Format("Intercepted a call to {0}", name))
      End If
   End Sub
End Class
```

Now, when we apply an attribute like this to a ContextBoundObject, all calls to methods on that object will trigger a message box.

Here is such a context-bound type:

```
<Logged()> Public Class LoggedObject
   Inherits ContextBoundObject

   Public Sub TestMethod()

   End Sub
End Class
```

It contains a sub that does nothing. Now, we can make a simple Windows application that instantiates a `LoggedObject`, and calls the `TestMethod` when we click a button. Drag a button onto a standard WinForm, and edit the code as follows:

```
Public Class Form1
   Inherits System.Windows.Forms.Form

   Private _obj As New LoggedObject()

' Windows Form Designer generated code

   Private Sub Button1_Click(ByVal sender As System.Object, _
               ByVal e As System.EventArgs) Handles Button1.Click
      _obj.TestMethod()
   End Sub
End Class
```

Now, when we click the button, the messagebox appears telling us it intercepted the call to a method on our logged class. This opens up a potentially powerful ability to attach functionality onto classes simply by decorating them with attributes, but does create a large overhead in object management through its reliance on the remoting model. In the absence of detailed Microsoft documentation, it is difficult to discover the real side effects of this technique.

Summary

Attributes play a vital role in a wide range of scenarios in .NET. As we've seen during the chapter, attribute classes inherit from `System.Attribute`, and are decorated with an `<AttributeUsage()>` attribute to define the applicability of the attribute class.

We can use reflection techniques to determine the standard and custom attributes defined on a particular target: to get the list of standard attributes defined on a type, use the `Attributes` property; to get the list of custom attributes defined on a type, use the `GetCustomAttributes()` method.

We've seen many uses of attributes during the chapter; here's a quick reminder of some of the attribute classes we've encountered:

❑   `<Serializable()>` indicates that a class, structure, enumeration, or delegate is serializable. `<NonSerialized()>` indicates a field should not be serialized.

❑   `<Conditional()>` indicates that a method is conditionally compiled. This attribute is commonly used to control how diagnostic information is displayed in a .NET application.

❑   `<AssemblyTitle()>`, `<AssemblyDescription()>`,
     `<AssemblyCompany()>`, `<AssemblyProduct()>`,
     `<AssemblyCopyright()>`, `<AssemblyTrademark()>` and
     `<AssemblyGuid()>` provide metadata for an entire assembly.

This is not a comprehensive list of attribute classes available in .NET. For a complete list, take a look at Attribute class, about Attribute class in Visual Studio .NET Help, and click on the hyperlink for Derived classes.

If none of these attribute classes meets your needs, you can of course define new custom attribute classes of your own. Choose a class name that ends with 'Attribute', and inherit from `System.Attribute`. Remember to provide an `<AttributeUsage()>` attribute to specify the applicability of your attribute class, and define suitable constructors and get/set properties to initialize attribute instances accordingly.

We also looked at some of the possibilities offered by the poorly documented context-bound attributes. The examples covered in this chapter should give you a good idea of what's possible using attributes in .NET.

The next chapter will look at how reflection and attributes empower a part of the .NET framework which defines and uses more attributes than any other – the component model.

VB.NET

Reflection

Handbook

6

6

The .NET Component Model

This is the final chapter in the book, and it gives us the opportunity to see how attributes, metadata, and reflection are used within the .NET Framework.

In this chapter, we'll investigate the various classes, interfaces, and other data types defined in the `System.ComponentModel` namespace. The .NET Component Model provides an extremely rich programming model for creating and using component classes. We'll explain exactly what we mean by a 'component class' shortly. The aim of the chapter is to show how we can use reflection and attribute-based techniques to write programs that are generic and can handle any kind of component. The chapter provides an effective case study in writing code that makes use of attribute-laden objects, and offers some insight into the way the developers at Microsoft have employed attributes within .NET.

This is a chapter of two halves:

❑   The first half of the chapter introduces the important interfaces, classes, and attributes in the `System.ComponentModel` namespace. We'll see how to use reflection to interrogate a type about its run time capabilities, such as obtaining a list of its properties and events. This enables us to write our code in a very flexible and extensible manner. Rather than constraining our applications to deal with specific types containing predefined properties and events, we can write generic code that determines these capabilities dynamically at runtime.

We'll also see how to determine whether a type can be converted to other data types by using a converter class. This is an essential ingredient if we want to use types generically in our application; we must be able to interrogate types to determine whether their data can be converted to or from other types. For example, the Visual Designer in Visual Studio .NET needs to be able to convert components' property values to and from string format, in order to display and edit these values in the Properties window.

❑	The second part of the chapter shows how to create new component classes, to take advantage of the rich set of attributes and other metadata capabilities defined in the System.ComponentModel namespace. We'll define a new component class, decorate it with attributes, and then add it to the Toolbox in Visual Studio .NET. Then we'll show how to drag-and-drop component objects onto a new application, and see how the Component Designer in Visual Studio .NET deals with these component objects. This will illustrate the power of attributed programming, and the use of reflection to determine a component's capabilities at runtime.

Let's begin with a tour of the .NET Component Model, to gain an understanding of the classes, interfaces, and attributes available to us.

Investigating the .NET Component Model

As its name suggests, the .NET Component Model is geared up for creating and using components. Therefore, a logical place for us to start is by defining exactly what we mean by a component. We'll also describe the differences between components, controls, and classes.

The component model defines a standard programming model for creating and using any kind of component in a .NET application. Attributes and reflection play a pivotal role in this programming model.

Components, Controls, and Classes

What exactly do we mean by a 'component'? Well, in traditional programming terminology, a component is a black box of compiled code, which hides its functionality behind a well-defined interface. COM components were always accessed through COM interfaces, regardless of the underlying programming technology. In .NET, pretty much any object is a component by this definition. A .NET component goes beyond the basics any object offers by providing:

❑	Simplified discovery of its capabilities via reflection

❑	Design-time support, allowing it to be configured by an IDE such as Visual Studio .NET

❑	A container architecture that enables components to discover and interact with one another

The strict definition of a component in .NET is that it's a class that implements the `System.ComponentModel.IComponent` interface, and which provides an accessible no-argument constructor. The `IComponent` interface defines a standard mechanism for placing component objects into a container. All component classes in the .NET Framework class library implement `IComponent`.

The `System.ComponentModel.IContainer` interface specifies the requirements for container classes, to ensure that all container classes provide a consistent mechanism for adding and removing components.

What does all this mean in practical terms? Components and containers allow us to write code in a generic fashion; we can write component classes that implement the `IComponent` interface, and then insert component objects into any container. Conversely, we can write container classes that implement the `IContainer` interface, and then add any kind of component object.

The `IComponent` and `IContainer` interfaces also make it possible for visual designers such as Visual Studio .NET to work with component objects. As we'll show later, it's easy to add a component class to the Visual Studio .NET Toolbox, and then drag-and-drop component objects onto the Visual Designer.

It is important to realize that the term 'containment' means logical containment rather than visual containment. Later in the chapter, we'll underline this assertion by defining a non-visual component class named `Employee`; we'll also define a corresponding non-visual container class named `EmployeeContainer`, to contain `Employee` component objects. This example will illustrate the use of containers and components as a way of organizing groups of objects in a collection, to satisfy a one-to-many relationship in an object-oriented design.

It is also possible to define components that can reside in Windows Forms or ASP.NET web pages. These kinds of components are generally referred to as **controls**. Controls can be non-visual, in which case they are really just specialized components, or visual, in which case they provide a user interface element. There are two ways to create a new control class, depending on whether we want to add the control to Windows Forms or ASP.NET web pages:

❑   To create a new Windows Forms control, define a class that inherits from `System.Windows.Forms.Control`. This class provides basic user interface capabilities for Windows Forms controls. `System.Windows.Forms.Control` inherits from `Component`, which provides a basic implementation of the `IComponent` interface.

❑   To create a non-visual ASP.NET web control, define a class that inherits from `System.Web.UI.Control`. This class implements the `IComponent` interface directly. To create a visual ASP.NET web control, define a class that inherits from `System.Web.UI.WebControls.WebControl`.

The following UML diagram shows the relationship between the classes and interfaces introduced in this section. For more information about control classes in Windows Forms and ASP.NET web pages, see `System.Windows.Forms.Control` or `System.Web.UI.Control` respectively in Visual Studio .NET Help.

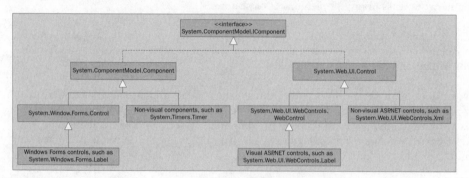

Using Reflection with the Component Model

The `System.ComponentModel` namespace provides a great deal of support for reflection, to enable the Visual Designer to interrogate the capabilities of components at design time. We can also use these reflection capabilities in our own programs at runtime, to find out anything we could ever want to know about types and objects in our program. We can also use reflection to modify property values, and even add new properties and events dynamically.

To illustrate how to use reflection with the Component Model, we'll present two sample applications:

❑   The first sample application will show how to use `System.ComponentModel.TypeDescriptor` to obtain general metadata for a component data type, such as the attributes defined on the type, and the default property and the default event for the type. The default property is the property that is initially highlighted in the Properties window when we select a component in the Visual Designer. The default event is the event that gets handled if we double-click a component in the Visual Designer; for example, the default event for `Button` is the `Click` event.

We'll also show how to retrieve further information about the properties and events on a specified type. Property information is represented by the `PropertyDescriptor` class, and event information is represented by the `EventDescriptor` class.

❑ The second sample application will show how to use reflection to dynamically modify properties at runtime. The application will allow us to select any property we like on a component, and change the property value on the fly. This illustrates the ability to deal with components in an entirely generic way, and reinforces the importance of attributes and reflection in this style of programming.

This task might sound like a trivial undertaking, but in fact it's a whole lot more complicated than you might imagine. Firstly, we'll need to use reflection to obtain the list of properties on the component. Then we'll need to use reflection to convert the user's new value into the correct data type for the property. This example will illustrate the true power of reflection, to write extremely generic code that works with any type of component.

Obtaining Metadata for Types, Properties, and Events

The `TypeDescriptor`, `EventDescriptor`, and `PropertyDescriptor` classes in the `System.ComponentModel` namespace provide us with a great deal of metadata information. The following console application shows how to use these classes to find metadata for any data type in any assembly. You can download this sample application from the `ch06\GetTypeInformation` download folder for this book.

Let's begin with the `Imports` statements for the sample application:

```
Imports System               ' For miscellaneous .NET types
Imports System.Reflection    ' For the Assembly class
Imports System.ComponentModel ' For the descriptor classes
Imports System.Collections   ' For the IEnumerator interface
```

The application begins by displaying a message on the console, to ask the user for the name of the assembly to load into the runtime. The application also asks the user for the name of a data type in the assembly, and gets a `Type` object for the requested type. The application then displays a menu on the console, offering the user a chance to display various aspects of metadata for the specified data type:

```
Public Class MainClass

    ' Helper variable
    Private Shared nl As String = System.Environment.NewLine

    Public Shared Sub Main()

        Try

            ' Ask the user for an assembly name
            Console.Write("Please enter the assembly name: ")
            Dim assemblyName As String = Console.ReadLine()
```

169

```
      ' Load the requested assembly into the runtime
      Dim theAssembly As [Assembly] = _
        [Assembly].LoadWithPartialName(assemblyName)
      Console.WriteLine("Loaded " & theAssembly.FullName & nl)

      ' Ask the user for a type name
      Console.Write("Please enter a fully-qualified type name: ")
      Dim typeName As String = Console.ReadLine()
      ' Get the Type object for this type
      Dim theType As Type = theAssembly.GetType(typeName, True, True)
      Console.WriteLine("Found the type " & theType.FullName & nl)

      ' Display a menu of options to the user
      Dim response As String
      Do
        Console.WriteLine("MAIN MENU, choose an option: ")
        Console.WriteLine("-----------------------------------------")
        Console.WriteLine("  t  Display general type information")
        Console.WriteLine("  e  Display all events for this type")
        Console.WriteLine("  p  Display all properties for this type")
        Console.WriteLine("  q  Quit")
        Console.WriteLine()
        Console.Write("> ")
        response = Console.ReadLine()

        ' Call appropriate method to display the requested information
        If response = "t" Then
          MyDisplayTypeInfo(theType)
        ElseIf response = "e" Then
          MyDisplayEventsInfo(theType)
        ElseIf response = "p" Then
          MyDisplayPropertiesInfo(theType)
        End If

      Loop Until response = "q"

    Catch Ex As Exception
      Console.WriteLine("Exception: " & Ex.Message & nl)
    End Try

  End Sub

  ' The methods MyDisplayTypeInfo(), MyDisplayEventsInfo(), and
  ' MyDisplayPropertiesInfo() are discussed below...

End Class
```

The following code shows the implementation of the MyDisplayTypeInfo() method, to display general metadata for the specified type. We use the TypeDescriptor class (defined in the System.ComponentModel namespace) to obtain this metadata:

1. Firstly, we call `TypeDescriptor.GetDefaultEvent()` to get information about the default event for the specified data type. The event information is returned in an `EventDescriptor` object, which contains information such as the name of the event.

The default event for a component is defined by the `<DefaultEvent()>` attribute on the component class definition. When we call `TypeDescriptor.GetDefaultEvent()`, the method returns the event specified by this attribute. We'll see how to use `<DefaultEvent()>` in the second part of the chapter, when we define a new component class of our own.

2. Next, we call `TypeDescriptor.GetDefaultProperty()` to get information about the default property for the specified data type. The property information is returned in a `PropertyDescriptor` object, which contains information such as the name of the property.

The default property for a component is defined by the `<DefaultProperty()>` attribute on the component class definition. We'll see how to use `<DefaultProperty()>` in the second part of the chapter.

3. Finally, we call `TypeDescriptor.GetAttributes()` to get the collection of attributes defined on the specified data type. We iterate through this collection, and display the name of each attribute on the console:

```
Public Shared Sub MyDisplayTypeInfo(ByVal theType As Type)

   Console.WriteLine(nl & "Type information for type {0}", _
                     theType.FullName)
   Console.WriteLine("-----------------------------------------------")

   ' Display name of default event (if there is one) for this type
   Dim defaultEvent As EventDescriptor
   defaultEvent = TypeDescriptor.GetDefaultEvent(theType)
   If defaultEvent Is Nothing Then
      Console.WriteLine("Default event:    none")
   Else
      Console.WriteLine("Default event:    {0}", defaultEvent.Name)
   End If

   ' Display name of default property (if there is one) for this type
   Dim defaultProperty As PropertyDescriptor
   defaultProperty = TypeDescriptor.GetDefaultProperty(theType)
   If defaultProperty Is Nothing Then
      Console.WriteLine("Default property: none")
   Else
      Console.WriteLine("Default property: {0}", defaultProperty.Name)
   End If
```

```
' Display the names of all the attributes defined on this type
Console.WriteLine("Attributes:")
Dim attribs As AttributeCollection
attribs = TypeDescriptor.GetAttributes(theType)
Dim iter As IEnumerator = attribs.GetEnumerator()
While iter.MoveNext
   Console.WriteLine("  {0}", iter.Current)
End While
Console.WriteLine()

End Sub
```

The following code shows the implementation of the `MyDisplayEventsInfo()` method.
The method calls `TypeDescriptor.GetEvents()`, to get the collection of events defined
in the specified type. We iterate through this collection, and display detailed information for
each event. The `EventDescriptor` class provides complete information about the event,
including: the name of the event; the delegate type of the event; a textual description of the
event; the category of the event when displayed in the Properties window; whether the
event is available only at design time; and whether the event is multicast (multiple listeners
supported) or single-cast (only one listener supported):

```
Public Shared Sub MyDisplayEventsInfo(ByVal theType As Type)

   Console.WriteLine(nl & "Event information")
   Console.WriteLine("----------------------------------------------------")

   ' Get descriptive information for all events defined in this type
   Dim eventDescriptors As EventDescriptorCollection
   eventDescriptors = TypeDescriptor.GetEvents(theType)

   ' Iterate through the events, and display info for each event
   Dim iter As IEnumerator = eventDescriptors.GetEnumerator()
   While iter.MoveNext

      Dim cur As EventDescriptor
      cur = CType(iter.Current, EventDescriptor)

      Console.WriteLine("Event Name:               {0}", cur.Name)
      Console.WriteLine("Event Type:               {0}", cur.EventType)
      Console.WriteLine("Event Description:        {0}", cur.Description)
      Console.WriteLine("Event Category:           {0}", cur.Category)
      Console.WriteLine("Event DesignTimeOnly:     {0}", cur.DesignTimeOnly)
      Console.WriteLine("Event IsBrowsable:        {0}", cur.IsBrowsable)
      Console.WriteLine("Event IsMulticast:        {0}", cur.IsMulticast)
      Console.WriteLine()

   End While

End Sub
```

To complete our sample application, the following code shows the implementation of `MyDisplayPropertiesInfo()`. This method is similar to `MyDisplayEventsInfo()` shown above; this time, we call `TypeDescriptor.GetProperties()` to get the collection of properties defined in the specified type, and iterate through the collection to display information for each property:

```
Public Shared Sub MyDisplayPropertiesInfo(ByVal theType As Type)

    Console.WriteLine(nl & "Property information")
    Console.WriteLine("-------------------------------------------------")

    ' Get descriptive information for all properties in this type
    Dim propDescriptors As PropertyDescriptorCollection
    propDescriptors = TypeDescriptor.GetProperties(theType)
    ' Iterate through the properties, and display info for each property
    Dim iter As IEnumerator = propDescriptors.GetEnumerator()
    While iter.MoveNext

        Dim cur As PropertyDescriptor
        cur = CType(iter.Current, PropertyDescriptor)

        Console.WriteLine("Property Name:          {0}", cur.Name)
        Console.WriteLine("Property Type:          {0}", cur.PropertyType)
        Console.WriteLine("Property Description:   {0}", cur.Description)
        Console.WriteLine("property Category:      {0}", cur.Category)
        Console.WriteLine("Property DesignTimeOnly:{0}", _
                                                cur.DesignTimeOnly)
        Console.WriteLine("Property IsBrowsable:   {0}", cur.IsBrowsable)
        Console.WriteLine("Property IsReadOnly:    {0}", cur.IsReadOnly)
        Console.WriteLine()

    End While

End Sub
```

When we build and run the application, it asks for an assembly name and a type name. We've specified the System assembly and the System.Timers.Timer component type, because it has a reasonably small number of events and properties. Feel free to choose a different assembly name and type name if you run this application yourself:

When we choose the t option, the application displays the following general type information for the Timer type. The default event is Elapsed, and the default property is Interval. There is a sizable list of attributes on the Timer class, and this is a hint of things to come. As you'll see later in the chapter, attributes play a major role in defining the design time and runtime capabilities of components. To corroborate this assertion, notice that most of the attributes displayed below are located in the System.ComponentModel namespace:

```
C:\Reflection\ch06\GetTypeInformation\bin\GetTypeInformation.exe

MAIN MENU, choose an option:
   t   Display general type information
   e   Display all events for this type
   p   Display all properties for this type
   q   Quit
> t
Type information for type System.Timers.Timer
---------------------------------------------------------
Default event:      Elapsed
Default property:   Interval
Attributes:
   System.ComponentModel.Design.Serialization.RootDesignerSerializerAttribute
   System.ComponentModel.DesignerAttribute
   System.ComponentModel.DesignerCategoryAttribute
   System.ComponentModel.DefaultEventAttribute
   System.Runtime.InteropServices.ComVisibleAttribute
   System.ComponentModel.DefaultPropertyAttribute
   System.ComponentModel.DesignerAttribute
   System.ComponentModel.TypeConverterAttribute
```

When we choose the e option, our application displays the following information about the events in the Timer type. The Name, Description, IsBrowsable, and Category information for each event is primarily intended for design time consumption by the Visual Designer (IsBrowsable indicates whether the event is viewable in the Visual Designer, and Category is used to group related events together in the Visual Designer). In contrast, the Type and IsMulticast information actually affect how the events behave at runtime. As this example illustrates, components must provide a suitable combination of design time and runtime metadata, to support the Visual Designer and the CLR respectively:

```
C:\Reflection\ch06\GetTypeInformation\bin\GetTypeInformation.exe

MAIN MENU, choose an option:
   t   Display general type information
   e   Display all events for this type
   p   Display all properties for this type
   q   Quit
> e
Event information
---------------------------------------------------------
Event Name:          Elapsed
Event Type:          System.Timers.ElapsedEventHandler
Event Description:   Occurs when the Interval has elapsed.
Event Category:      Behavior
Event DesignTimeOnly: False
Event IsBrowsable:   True
Event IsMulticast:   True

Event Name:          Disposed
Event Type:          System.EventHandler
Event Description:
Event Category:      Misc
Event DesignTimeOnly: False
Event IsBrowsable:   False
Event IsMulticast:   True
```

To conclude this example, let's see what happens when we choose the p option in our application. The following information is displayed for the properties in the Timer type; we've only listed the first few properties here:

Let's briefly summarize what we've learnt in this example. The
`System.ComponentModel` namespace contains the descriptor classes
`TypeDescriptor`, `EventDescriptor`, and `PropertyDescriptor`, to provide full
and detailed metadata for data types, events, and properties. This metadata is defined
using a wide range of attributes, most of which are also defined in the
`System.ComponentModel` namespace. We'll see how to use these attributes later in
the chapter.

Using Metadata to Write Generic Code

The previous example showed how to query the metadata in types, events, and
properties. It's also possible to use this metadata to change the state of objects at
runtime. The metadata provides all the information we need to manipulate any kind of
component; we can write generic code that can happily deal with any members on any
type of component. Rather than restricting ourselves to using hard-coded property
names and event names, we can use reflection to determine these features dynamically.
This means we can write applications that are flexible enough to deal with component
types that didn't even exist when we first wrote our code; our applications are resilient
enough to detect the types and capabilities of these new components at runtime.

One of the exciting possibilities with this style of programming is the ability to write
pluggable software. Our software can dynamically load any kind of component, maybe
based on locale or user details, and interact with these components via reflection.

This sounds almost too good to be true, doesn't it? Where's the catch? Well, as is
usually the case, it's more difficult to write generic code than it is to write code for a
specific component, event, or property. We have to work a bit harder to discover the
information that we need to achieve our task. Furthermore, using reflection can cause
inefficiencies at runtime, due to the extra effort our application has to expend to access
the required metadata. However, the overall effect is worth the effort, as you'll see in
the following application.

The sample application for this section of the chapter appears as follows. You can download this Windows Forms application from the ch06\GenericProgramming download folder:

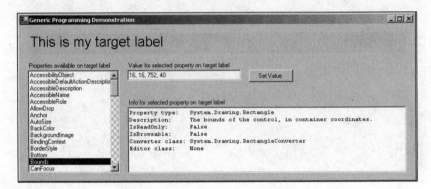

The application allows the user to dynamically change any property on the upper label component on the form. Here is a list of the components in the form:

Component type	Component name
System.Windows.Forms.Label	lblTarget
System.Windows.Forms.ListBox	lstProperties
System.Windows.Forms.TextBox	txtNewValue
System.Windows.Forms.Button	btnSetValue
System.Windows.Forms.RichTextBox	txtInfo

The main Visual Basic source file in the application has the following Imports statements:

```
Imports System                     ' For general .NET types
Imports System.Windows.Forms       ' For general Windows Forms types
Imports System.Drawing.Design       ' For the UIEditor class (see later)
Imports System.ComponentModel      ' For the .NET Component Model types
```

This is how the application works:

❑ When the form loads, the application uses reflection to get the list of available properties for the label component, lblTarget. These properties are displayed in the list box on the left-hand side of the form, lstProperties. The following code shows these tasks:

```
Private Sub Form1_Load(ByVal sender As System.Object, _
                  ByVal e As System.EventArgs) _
              Handles MyBase.Load

  ' Get descriptive information for all the properties on lblTarget
  Dim propDescriptors As PropertyDescriptorCollection
  propDescriptors = TypeDescriptor.GetProperties(Me.lblTarget)

  ' Display each property in the ListBox, lstProperties
  Dim I As Integer
  For I = 0 To propDescriptors.Count - 1
    Me.lstProperties.Items.Add(propDescriptors(I).Name)
  Next

End Sub
```

❏ The code below shows what happens when the user selects a property in
   the list box. The application uses reflection to get further information for
   the selected property, and displays this information in the large text area in
   the lower-right hand corner of the form. The property information includes:

   • The data type of the property. For example, the data type of the
      Bounds property is displayed as System.Drawing.Rectangle in the
      previous screenshot.

   • A textual description of the property. Components provide this
      information for the benefit of the Visual Designer.

   • A flag that indicates whether the property is read-only. For example, the
      previous screenshot showed that the Bounds property is not read-only.

   • A flag that indicates whether the property is browsable at design time.
      For example, the previous screenshot showed that the Bounds
      property is not browsable at design time. In other words, the Bounds
      property will not be displayed in the Properties window in the Visual
      Designer; the Bounds property is only usable at runtime.

   • The name of a converter class associated with the data type of this
      property. For example, the previous screenshot showed that the
      converter class for the Bounds property is
      System.Drawing.RectangleConverter. This converter class
      converts Rectangle objects to strings and vice versa, to allow the value
      to be edited as a string in the Properties window in Visual Studio .NET.
      The .NET Framework class library provides a suite of converter classes,
      all inherited from System.ComponentModel.TypeConverter, whose
      purpose is to convert values to and from other data types.

- The name of an editor class associated with the data type of this property. Editor classes are provided by the .NET Framework, to help the user edit non-trivial data types such as Font, DateTime, and Color. To get the editor for the selected property's type, we call the TypeDescriptor.GetEditor() method. This method requires two parameters: the data type of the property; and the base data type for the editor. UITypeEditor is the base class for all the editor classes in .NET; all editor classes inherit from UITypeEditor. If you take another look at the screenshot we showed earlier, you'll notice that there is no editor class associated with the Bounds property; this means Rectangle values must be edited directly in string format (for example, 16, 16, 752, 40).

The application also gets the current value of the selected property, and uses the appropriate converter class (such as System.Drawing.RectangleConverter) to convert this value into a string. Later in the chapter, we'll see how the Visual Designer ascertains which converter class to use for each property. The string value of the property is displayed in the small text field in the middle of the form.

```
' Helper variable
Private nl As String = Environment.NewLine

' Remember property information for the currently-selected property
Private mSelectedProp As PropertyDescriptor

' Remember the TypeConverter for the currently-selected property
Private mConverter As TypeConverter


Private Sub lstProperties_SelectedIndexChanged( _
                                ByVal sender As Object, _
                                ByVal e As System.EventArgs) _
                    Handles lstProperties.SelectedIndexChanged

  ' Get the selected property in the lstProperties Listbox
  Dim selectedPropName As String = Me.lstProperties.SelectedItem

  ' Get the PropertyDescriptor for the selected property
  Dim propDescriptors As PropertyDescriptorCollection
  propDescriptors = TypeDescriptor.GetProperties(Me.lblTarget)
  Me.mSelectedProp = propDescriptors.Find(selectedPropName, False)

  ' Use the PropertyDescriptor to display simple info for the property
  Me.txtInfo.Clear()
  Me.txtInfo.AppendText("Property type:   " & _
                    Me.mSelectedProp.PropertyType.ToString() & nl)
  Me.txtInfo.AppendText("Description:     " & _
                    Me.mSelectedProp.Description & nl)
  Me.txtInfo.AppendText("IsReadOnly:      " & _
                    Me.mSelectedProp.IsReadOnly & nl)
```

```
   Me.txtInfo.AppendText("IsBrowsable:     " & _
                       Me.mSelectedProp.IsBrowsable & nl)

   ' Can this property be modified in string format?
   ' Assume it can't, for now...
   Dim canModifyFlag As Boolean = False

   ' Display info about the property's type-converter class
   Me.mConverter = Me.mSelectedProp.Converter
   If Me.mConverter Is Nothing Then
     Me.txtInfo.AppendText("Converter class: None" & nl)
   ElseIf Me.mConverter.CanConvertFrom(GetType(String)) = False Then
     Me.txtInfo.AppendText("Converter class: " & _
                       "Cannot convert from string value" & nl)
   Else
     Me.txtInfo.AppendText("Converter class: " & _
                         Me.mConverter.GetType().ToString() & nl)
     If Not Me.mSelectedProp.IsReadOnly Then
       canModifyFlag = True
     End If
   End If

   ' Enable or disable editing of the property's value
   Me.txtNewValue.Enabled = canModifyFlag
   Me.btnSetValue.Enabled = canModifyFlag

   ' Display current value of property (if expressable as a string)
   If (Me.mConverter Is Nothing) Or _
      (Me.mConverter.CanConvertTo(GetType(String))) = False Then
     Me.txtNewValue.Text = ""
   Else
     Dim objValue As Object
     objValue = Me.mSelectedProp.GetValue(Me.lblTarget)
     Dim strValue As String
     strValue = Me.mConverter.ConvertTo(objValue, GetType(String))
     Me.txtNewValue.Text = strValue
   End If

   ' Display info about the property's editor class
   Dim editor As Object
   editor = TypeDescriptor.GetEditor(Me.mSelectedProp.PropertyType, _
                         GetType(UITypeEditor))
   If editor Is Nothing Then
     Me.txtInfo.AppendText("Editor class:    None" & nl)
   Else
     Me.txtInfo.AppendText("Editor class:    " & _
                       editor.GetType().ToString() & nl)
   End If

End Sub
```

❏   The application allows the user to type in a new value for the property.
    When the user clicks the Set Value button, the application gets the string
    value entered by the user, and converts it into the appropriate data type for
    the property. To achieve this conversion, the application uses the
    appropriate conversion class for the property in question.

```
Private Sub btnSetValue_Click(ByVal sender As System.Object, _
                        ByVal e As System.EventArgs) _
                Handles btnSetValue.Click

    Try
        ' Get the property value entered in the TextBox, txtNewValue
        Dim strValue As String = Me.txtNewValue.Text

        ' Use the PropertyDescriptor for the selected property,
        ' to convert the string into the correct type for the property
        Dim objValue As Object = Me.mConverter.ConvertFrom(strValue)

        ' Set the property on the Label, lblTarget
        Me.mSelectedProp.SetValue(Me.lblTarget, objValue)

    Catch Ex As Exception
        MessageBox.Show(Ex.Message, _
                    "Exception occurred", _
                    MessageBoxButtons.OK, _
                    MessageBoxIcon.Error)
    End Try

End Sub
```

Let's build and run the application, to see what we can do. When the application form
appears, make some changes to the properties of the target label. Here are some
suggestions, but feel free to experiment with your own property changes:

Property	New value for property
BackColor	DarkBlue
Font	Tahoma, 20pt
ForeColor	255, 122, 78
Height	32
Left	50
RightToLeft	Yes
Text	This is my new label text
Width	500

If you make the changes we've suggested, the target label will appear as follows on the form:

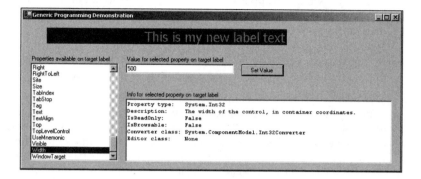

Creating New Components

Now that we've seen how to use reflection to access metadata for predefined .NET components, let's consider how to write new components of our own. This will consolidate our understanding of how components work, and provide a deeper insight into the role of attributes and other data types defined in the System.ComponentModel namespace.

Once we've written our components, developers will be able to use our components just like they use standard components defined in the .NET Framework class library. For example, developers will be able to add our components to the Toolbox in Visual Studio .NET, and drag-and-drop component objects onto the Visual Designer. This helps developers to build applications quickly and (relatively) effortlessly, by plugging together prefabricated components and using their functionality as required.

We'll tackle the following tasks in this section of the chapter:

❑ We'll begin by defining a simple component class named Employee. Along the way, we'll present various guidelines for defining 'good' component classes.

❑ Once we've written our embryonic version of the Employee component class, we'll show how to store components in a container. The System.ComponentModel namespace has an interface named IContainer, which defines the basic requirements for container classes. To simplify application development, there is also a standard class named Container, which provides a base implementation of IContainer. We'll see how to use Container to hold Employee component instances. We'll also see how to write a custom container class by implementing IContainer directly, which is a useful approach if we need more functionality than is provided by the standard Container class.

❑ It's also possible to host components in Windows Forms and ASP.NET web pages, by adding our component class to the Toolbox in Visual Studio .NET. This will allow application developers to drag-and-drop `Employee` component objects onto the Visual Designer, in the same way as they can drag-and-drop predefined components such as `System.Windows.Forms.Timer` and `System.Data.SqlClient.SqlConnection`. We'll take a look at the code that gets generated when we add component objects to an application.

❑ Our next task will be to add properties and events to our `Employee` component class. We'll annotate these properties and events with attributes, to enable Visual Studio .NET to display these members properly at design time. For example, we'll use the `<Description()>` attribute to define a textual description for each property in `Employee`. We'll also use the `<Category()>` attribute to group related properties into categories.

We'll also see how these attributes affect the code that gets generated when we add `Employee` component objects to a host application.

❑ To close the chapter, we'll show how to write converter classes for an `Address` class and a `TelephoneNumber` class. The converter classes will enable `Address` and `TelephoneNumber` objects to be converted to strings, and vice versa. We'll see how the Visual Designer uses these converter classes to allow the user to modify complex properties in the Properties window at design time.

By the end of this section, we'll have built a fully functional component class that exhibits many of the characteristics found in standard .NET component classes. If you want to skip ahead, you can download a complete and working version of this component class from the download folder `ch06\MyFinalComponent`. You can also download a sample application that uses this component; see the download folder `ch06\UseFinalComponent`.

Defining a Component Class

As we described at the beginning of the chapter, a component class is simply a class that implements the `IComponent` interface. There is another technical constraint we haven't mentioned yet: component classes must either provide a no-argument constructor, or a constructor that takes a single parameter of type `IContainer`.

The easiest way to implement the `IComponent` interface is to inherit it directly or indirectly from one of the following:

❑ `System.ComponentModel.Component`. This class provides a base implementation of the IComponent interface, suitable for marshal-by-reference components. If we pass an instance of any marshal-by-reference class into a method on a remote server, the CLR passes an object reference rather than a copy of the object. For more information about .NET Remoting, see Wrox' VB.NET Remoting Handbook (ISBN 1861007-40-X).

❑ `System.ComponentModel.MarshalByValueComponent`. As its name suggests, this class provides a base implementation of `IComponent` suitable for marshal-by-value components. If we pass an instance of a marshal-by-value component into a method on a remote server, the CLR passes a copy of the object rather than an object reference. Marshal-by-value types are typically used to represent data-laden objects that are passed back and forth between the client and server in a .NET Remoting application.

❑ `System.Web.UI.Control`. This class defines the methods, properties, and events that are common for all ASP.NET server controls. Note that the equivalent base class for Windows Forms controls, `System.Windows.Forms.Control`, extends `Component` rather than implementing `IComponent` directly.

❑ `System.Web.HttpApplication`. This class will be of interest to you if you are familiar with ASP.NET and web applications. The `HttpApplication` class defines the methods, properties, and events that are common for all ASP.NET application objects defined in a `Global.asax` file in a web application. Application objects provide information and services that are shared and accessed by all users of a web application, rather than for a specific session (session-specific state is maintained in an `HttpSessionState` object).

When we write a component class, the first step is to choose an appropriate access modifier for the component class. The choices are the same as for a normal class:

❑ If we want the component to be available to all client applications, we must define the accessibility of the component class as `Public`:

```
' This component can be accessed anywhere
Public Class Employee
    Inherits System.ComponentModel.Component

    ' Members ...

End Class
```

❑ If we want the component to be available only to other code in the same assembly, we can declare the accessibility as `Friend`. This is the default accessibility if we do not specify any accessibility specifiers:

```
' This component can only be accessed by code in the same assembly
Friend Class Employee
   Inherits System.ComponentModel.Component

   ' Members ...

End Class
```

❑ If we want the component to be available only to a specific class, we can define the component class as a nested class as shown below (nested classes are often referred to as inner classes in other object-oriented programming languages). We can use the `Private`, `Protected`, `Friend`, or `Protected Friend` accessibility modifiers to control the accessibility of the nested component:

```
Public Class MyOuterClass

   ' This component can only be accessed by MyOuterClass, because we've
   ' used the Private access modifier. Alternatively, we can specify:
   '    Protected (accessible by derived classes)
   '    Friend (accessible by classes in the same assembly)
   '    Protected Friend (combination of Protected and Friend access)
   Private Class Employee
      Inherits System.ComponentModel.Component

      ' Members ...

   End Class

End Class
```

Another important issue is to specify a meaningful namespace and assembly information for our component. This is especially important if we intend our component to be used widely by other developers, in order to avoid name clashes with any other components these developers might be using. If we want to allow developers to drag-and-drop instances of our component onto their applications from the Visual Studio .NET Toolbox, we need to provide as much useful information as we can about our component.

To define a component class, we can either type all the source code into a text editor such as Notepad, or we can use Visual Studio .NET to help generate some of the boilerplate code. We'll take the latter approach, but we'll also show all the generated code to prove there's nothing magical happening under the covers.

To create a template component class in Visual Studio .NET, follow these steps:

❑ Create a new project containing a Visual Basic .NET class library. Choose a meaningful name for the project, such as MyComponent.

184

❏ Visual Studio .NET generates a mostly-empty class file named Class1.vb. Right-click on this filename in Solution Explorer, and select Delete from the shortcut menu. We won't be using this file.

❏ In Solution Explorer, right-click the project name (MyComponent in this example) and select Add | Add New Item from the shortcut menu. The Add New Item dialog box appears; click Component Class from the Templates list, and enter a suitable name for the component class. For this example, enter the filename Employee.vb. Then click Open.

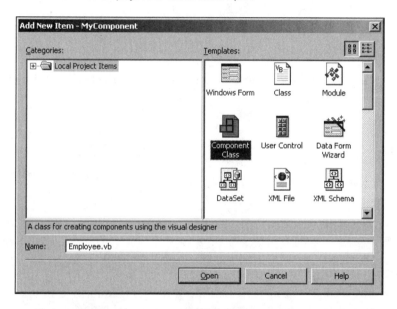

The Component Designer in Visual Studio .NET generates starter source code in Employee.vb, to define a simple component class. Let's dissect this code, and investigate the component-related features.

❏ Firstly, the new class inherits from System.ComponentModel.Component as expected:

```
Imports System
Imports System.ComponentModel

Public Class Employee
   Inherits System.ComponentModel.Component

   ' Members...

End Class
```

If we want a marshal-by-value component rather than a marshal-by-reference component, all we have to do is change the superclass from `Component` to `MarshalByValueComponent` as follows:

```
' This is a marshal-by-value component class
Public Class Employee
    Inherits System.ComponentModel.MarshalByValueComponent

    ' Members...

End Class
```

❏ The `Employee` component class contains two constructors, generated by the Component Designer. These constructors are in the `Component Designer` generated code region in the `Employee` class. The first constructor takes an `IContainer` parameter, which represents the logical container of the component. The constructor calls the no-arg constructor (discussed next), and then adds the current component (me) to the container:

```
Public Sub New(Container As System.ComponentModel.IContainer)

    ' Call the no-arg constructor (see below)
    MyClass.New()

    'Required for Windows.Forms Class Composition Designer support
    Container.Add(me)

End Sub
```

The second constructor is shown below. This constructor calls the base-class constructor, and then calls a helper method named `InitializeComponent()` to initialize this component. The code in `InitializeComponent()` is generated automatically by the Component Designer, so we must not edit the code in `InitializeComponent()` directly. Instead, if we have any additional initialization to perform for our component, we should add code at the end of the constructor as indicated by the final comment:

```
Public Sub New()

    ' Call the base-class constructor
    MyBase.New()

    'This call is required by the Component Designer.
    InitializeComponent()

    'Add any initialization after the InitializeComponent() call

End Sub
```

❑ The `InitializeComponent()` method is shown below, along with the definition of an `IContainer` field named `components`. The `InitializeComponent()` method creates a new `Container` object and assigns it to the `components` field as follows:

```
'Required by the Component Designer
Private components As System.ComponentModel.IContainer

'NOTE: The following procedure is required by the Component Designer
'It can be modified using the Component Designer.
'Do not modify it using the code editor.
<System.Diagnostics.DebuggerStepThrough()>_
Private Sub InitializeComponent()

    components = New System.ComponentModel.Container()

End Sub
```

This arrangement allows our component to itself act as a container for other components. For example, if we viewed our component in Design View, we could add other components to it from the Toolbox or Server Explorer, such as timer components, MSMQ components, database connection components, and so on.

❑ Our component class has a `Dispose()` method as shown below, to dispose of the additional components owned by our component. This `Dispose()` method overrides `Dispose()` in the base class, `Component`. The `Component` class implements `IDisposable`, which means all components exhibit disposable behavior. This means we can call `Dispose()` on any component object, to deterministically dispose of its sub-components.

```
Protected Overloads Overrides Sub Dispose(ByVal disposing As Boolean)

    If disposing Then
        If Not (components Is Nothing) Then
            components.Dispose()
        End If
    End If

    MyBase.Dispose(disposing)

End Sub
```

Our project also has an `AssemblyInfo.vb` source file, which contains a set of assembly attributes to define metadata for our assembly. Let's define some (reasonably) meaningful assembly attributes, as follows. For more about assembly attributes, see Chapter 5.

```
Imports System.Reflection
Imports System.Runtime.InteropServices

' General Information about an assembly is controlled through the
' following set of attributes. Change these attribute values to modify
' the information associated with an assembly.

' Review the values of the assembly attributes
<Assembly: AssemblyTitle("My assembly")>
<Assembly: AssemblyDescription("This assembly contains my component")>
<Assembly: AssemblyCompany("My Company")>
<Assembly: AssemblyProduct("")>
<Assembly: AssemblyCopyright("")>
<Assembly: AssemblyTrademark("")>
<Assembly: CLSCompliant(True)>

' The following GUID is for the ID of the typelib if this project
' is exposed to COM
<Assembly: Guid("837D85C8-C217-4FB6-A1E3-D3DCDF8E1C25")>

' Version information for an assembly consists of four values:
'
'       Major Version
'       Minor Version
'       Build Number
'       Revision
'
' You can specify all the values or you can default the Build and
' Revision Numbers by using the '*' syntax:

<Assembly: AssemblyVersion("1.0.0.0")>
```

If you are following these steps on your own computer, build the component in Visual Studio .NET to produce an assembly named `MyComponent.dll`. Later in the chapter, we'll see how to add this component to the Toolbox in Visual Studio .NET, and drag-and-drop component instances into a sample application.

Storing Components in a Container

As we described earlier in the chapter, the primary difference between component classes (that is, classes that implement `IComponent`) and other classes is that components possess the ability to be logically stored in containers. The `System.ComponentModel` namespace defines a standard class named `Container`, which implements `IContainer` and provides methods to add, remove, and retrieve components in a container. In many cases, the `Container` class is sufficient and there is no need to write our own custom class to implement `IContainer` directly.

Before we dive into the technicalities, let's just remind ourselves of the motivation for developing and using components and containers. We write components in order to provide chunks of functionality that we can leverage later in our project (and other developers can leverage in their projects); components provide a very effective way of building reusable software. Furthermore, because Visual Basic .NET is a .NET-compliant language, we can even reuse our components in other .NET-compliant languages such as Visual C# and Managed Extensions for C++. For example, we can write a container object that can hold components written in any .NET language.

Using the Standard Container Class to Host Components

To show how to use the standard `Container` class to hold components, we've provided a sample application in the `ch06\MySimpleContainer` download folder. The application uses an enhanced version of the `Employee` class that holds some employee data, and also provides an `Equals()` method to compare `Employee` objects to see if they hold the same employee data. This source code is located in the file `Employee.vb`:

```
Imports System
Imports System.ComponentModel

Public Class Employee
    Inherits System.ComponentModel.Component

    ' Some simple data for this employee
    Private mFullName As String

    ' Constructor, to initialize the data for this employee
    Public Sub New(ByVal FullName As String)
        mFullName = FullName
    End Sub

    ' Property to get the employee's full name
    Public ReadOnly Property FullName() As String
        Get
            Return mFullName
        End Get
    End Property

    ' Override Equals(), to compare two Employee objects for equality
    Public Overloads Function Equals(ByVal other As Object) As Boolean
        Dim otherEmp As Employee = CType(other, Employee)
        If mFullName = otherEmp.mFullName Then
            Return True
        Else
            Return False
        End If
    End Function

#Region " Component Designer generated code "
    ' Same as before...
#End Region

End Class
```

The Main() method for this sample application is located in a file named MainClass.vb. The full source code for the method is shown below.

The Main method begins by creating an instance of the standard Container class, and then creates four Employee component objects. To insert a component into a container, we call the Add() method on the container object. Add() takes two arguments: the component we want to insert; and a site name that uniquely identifies each component in this container. We'll discuss the role of site names in container classes shortly, when we discuss how to write our own custom container classes. In this example, we use an employee's ID number as the unique site name for each employee. Notice the last call to Add() will fail deliberately, because the site name "003" is already in use.

The Container class also has a Remove() method, which allows us to remove a component from a container. By default, Remove() compares object references to locate the object to remove; when we write our own custom container class shortly, we'll see how to compare object values by calling the Equals() method on Employee objects.

If we want to access the components in a container, we use the Components property as shown at the bottom of the Main() method. The Components property returns a ComponentCollection object, and we use an enumerator object to iterate through the components in this collection:

```vb
Imports System
Imports System.Collections
Imports System.ComponentModel

Public Class MainClass

  Public Shared Sub Main()

    ' Create a standard Container instance
    Dim firm As New Container()

    ' Create some components
    Dim emp1 As New Employee("Roger Smith")
    Dim emp2 As New Employee("Emily Jones")
    Dim emp3 As New Employee("Tommy Evans")
    Dim emp4 As New Employee("Hazel Ellis")

    Try
      ' Add components to the container. The last statement will fail
      ' deliberately, because the site name "003" is already in use.
      firm.Add(emp1, "001")
      firm.Add(emp2, "002")
      firm.Add(emp3, "003")
      firm.Add(emp4, "003")
    Catch e As SystemException
```

```
        Console.WriteLine("Exception: " + e.Message)
    End Try

    ' Remove an employee
    firm.Remove(emp1)

    ' Get a collection of all the components in the container
    Dim allEmps As ComponentCollection = firm.Components

    ' Loop through the component collection, and display each employee
    Dim iter As IEnumerator = allEmps.GetEnumerator()
    While (iter.MoveNext())
        Dim emp As Employee = CType(iter.Current, Employee)
        Console.WriteLine("Employee name: " + emp.FullName)
    End While

    End Sub

End Class
```

When we build and run the application, it displays the following messages on the console. These messages confirm that the first three `Employee` components were successfully inserted into the container, but the fourth `Employee` component failed due to a duplicate site name. The console messages also confirm that the employee "Roger Smith" was successfully removed from the container:

Defining a Custom Container Class to Host Components

On occasions, it may be necessary to write a custom container class that provides more specialized business logic than the predefined `Container` class. For example, we might want to write a container class that logs all insertions and removals to a Windows log file, or creates a backup copy of all removed objects in a database.

Whatever our motivation, there are two distinct steps when we define a custom container class:

❏   Define a class that implements the `ISite` interface, to associate a component object and a container object.

❏   Define a class that implements the `IContainer` interface, to manage the insertion, removal, and retrieval of components.

We've provided a sample application in the ch06\MyComplexContainer download folder, to illustrate these tasks.

Let's begin with the ISite interface. The ISite interface specifies the following members, to associate a component with a container. ISite also allows us to get or set a site name for each component in the container, and to query whether we're currently in design mode:

```
' This is the standard ISite interface in the .NET class library
Public Interface ISite
  Inherits IServiceProvider

  ' Property to get the component for this site
  Public ReadOnly Property Component() As IComponent

  ' Property to get the container for this site
  Public ReadOnly Property Container() As IContainer

  ' Property to indicate whether we're in design mode
  Public ReadOnly Property DesignMode() As Boolean

  ' Property to get/set the name of this site
  Public Property Name() As String

  ' Get the service for this site (inherited from IServiceProvider)
  Public Function GetService(ByVal serviceType As Type) As Object

End Interface
```

The following code shows how to implement the ISite interface, to associate Employee components with their container. This is a fairly generic implementation, and should suffice for most occasions where you need to implement the ISite interface. This code is available in the file EmployeeSite.vb.

Notice that all references to component objects are expressed using the interface type IComponent, rather than a specific component class such as EmployeeComponent. We have to use generic interface types, in order to comply with method signatures in the ISite interface. Similarly, all references to container objects are expressed using the interface type IContainer, rather than a specific container class such as EmployeeContainer. Despite this loss of strong type information at compile time, we can still discover everything we need about the component and container classes at runtime by using reflection, as we saw earlier in the chapter:

```
Imports System
Imports System.ComponentModel

Class EmployeeSite
  Implements ISite
```

```vb
' A site object associates a container with a component
Private mTheContainer As IContainer
Private mTheComponent As IComponent

' A site object uses a unique site name for each component in a
' container. Because we're in the EmployeeSite class, we'll use the
' employee's ID as the site name.
Private mEmpID As String

' Constructor, to associate a container with a component
Public Sub New(ByVal TheContainer As IContainer, _
               ByVal TheComponent As IComponent)
   mTheContainer = TheContainer
   mTheComponent = TheComponent
   mEmpID = Nothing
End Sub

' Property to get the component for this site
Public ReadOnly Property Component() As IComponent _
                     Implements ISite.Component
   Get
      Return mTheComponent
   End Get
End Property

' Property to get the container for this site
Public ReadOnly Property Container() As IContainer _
                     Implements ISite.Container
   Get
      Return mTheContainer
   End Get
End Property

' Property to indicate whether we're in design mode
' (always return False in this example - we're never in design mode)
Public ReadOnly Property DesignMode() As Boolean _
                     Implements ISite.DesignMode
   Get
      Return False
   End Get
End Property

' Property to get/set the name of this site
Public Property Name() As String Implements ISite.Name
   Get
      Return mEmpID
   End Get
   Set(ByVal Value As String)
      mEmpID = Value
   End Set
End Property
```

193

```
' Function to get the service for this site
' (inherited from IServiceProvider)
Public Function GetService(ByVal serviceType As Type) As Object _
                          Implements ISite.GetService
    Return Nothing
End Function

End Class
```

Now let's turn our attention to the IContainer interface. The IContainer interface specifies the following methods and properties, to insert, remove, and retrieve components in a container. Also, because IContainer inherits from the IDisposable interface, IContainer has a Dispose() method to perform deterministic destruction of the container:

```
' This is the standard IContainer interface in the .NET class library

Public Interface IContainer
    Inherits IDisposable

    ' Add a component (without specifying a Site name)
    Public Sub Add(ByVal aComponent As IComponent)

    ' Add a component (specifying a Site name)
    Public Sub Add(ByVal aComponent As IComponent, _
            ByVal SiteName As String)

    ' Remove the specified component from the container
    Public Sub Remove(ByVal emp As IComponent)

    ' Return all the components, wrapped up in a ComponentCollection
    Public ReadOnly Property Components() As ComponentCollection

    ' Dispose all components in container (inherited from IDisposable)
    Public Sub Dispose()

End Interface
```

The following sections of code show how to implement the IContainer interface, to contain Employee components. This implementation is also fairly generic, and should provide a good starting point if you need to implement the IContainer interface yourself some day. This code is available in the file EmployeeContainer.vb.

We've decided to use an ArrayList to store the Employee components, because it's easy to insert and remove items in an ArrayList:

```
Imports System
Imports System.ComponentModel
Imports System.Collections
```

```
Class EmployeeContainer
  Implements IContainer

  ' Hold a collection of Employee objects
  Private mEmployees As New ArrayList()

  ' Plus other members (see below...)

End Class
```

Here are the two overloaded Add() methods for our container class:

❑   The first Add() method adds the specified component to the ArrayList.
    No site name is specified for the new component, so we don't create an
    EmployeeSite object for this component. Without an EmployeeSite
    object, the component has no way of accessing its container object, should
    it need to do so:

```
Public Sub Add(ByVal emp As IComponent) Implements IContainer.Add
  mEmployees.Add(emp)
End Sub
```

❑   The second Add() method receives a site name for the new component.
    We test that the site name isn't already in use by an existing component in
    the container, and then insert the new component into the ArrayList. We
    also create a new Site object to remember the container object, the
    component object, and the component's site name:

```
Public Sub Add(ByVal emp As IComponent, ByVal empID As String) _
                        Implements IContainer.Add

  ' Loop through components, to see if the site name is already in use
  Dim i As Integer
  For i = 0 To mEmployees.Count - 1
    Dim cur As IComponent = CType(mEmployees(i), IComponent)
    If (Not cur.Site Is Nothing) And (cur.Site.Name = empID) Then
      Throw New SystemException("Employee ID " & empID & _
                        " already exists in container")
    End If
  Next

  ' Site name is OK, so add the component to the container
  mEmployees.Add(emp)

  ' Create a Site object to associate the container and the component
  Dim theSite As EmployeeSite = New EmployeeSite(Me, emp)
  theSite.Name = empID
  emp.Site = theSite

End Sub
```

Now let's see the `Remove()` method. `Remove()` receives a component as a parameter, and loops through all the components in the `ArrayList` searching for a match. The equality test is performed by calling the `Equals()` method defined in `Employee`, to compare the value of `Employee` objects rather than comparing object references (as was the case with the standard `Container` class earlier). If a matching `Employee` object is found, it is removed from the `ArrayList`:

```
Public Sub Remove(ByVal emp As IComponent) _
                        Implements IContainer.Remove

   Dim i As Integer
   Dim cur As Employee = CType(emp, Employee)

   ' Find a matching component in the container, and then remove it
   For i = 0 To mEmployees.Count - 1
      If cur.Equals(mEmployees(i)) Then
         mEmployees.RemoveAt(i)
         Exit For
      End If
   Next

End Sub
```

Moving swiftly on, the `EmployeeContainer` class also has a `Components` property as shown below. This property returns a `ComponentCollection` object, containing all the components held in the `ArrayList`:

```
Public ReadOnly Property Components() As ComponentCollection _
                        Implements IContainer.Components

   Get
      Dim componentArray(mEmployees.Count - 1) As IComponent
      mEmployees.CopyTo(componentArray)
      Return New ComponentCollection(componentArray)
   End Get

End Property
```

Finally, here is the code for the `Dispose()` method. This method disposes of each component, and then empties the `ArrayList`:

```
Public Sub Dispose() Implements IContainer.Dispose

   Dim i As Integer
   For i = 0 To mEmployees.Count - 1
      Dim cur As IComponent = mEmployees(i)
      cur.Dispose()
   Next

   mEmployees.Clear()

End Sub
```

To test the custom container class, we can use the same `Main()` method as before. The only difference is that we create an `EmployeeContainer` object, rather than a standard `Container` object:

```
Dim firm As New EmployeeContainer()
```

When we build and run the application, it displays the same messages as before. However, our application offers us much more flexibility than before; we can enhance the `EmployeeSite` and `EmployeeContainer` classes to perform additional business processing as needed.

```
C:\Reflection\ch06\MyComplexContainer\bin\MyComplexContainer.exe
Exception: Employee ID 003 already exists in container
Employee name: Emily Jones
Employee name: Tommy Evans
Press any key to continue_
```

Using Components in Visual Studio .NET

In the previous section, we saw how to use the `Container` class to manage collections of components. We also saw how to write a custom container class, to take greater control over how components are stored, retrieved, and removed.

In this section, we'll change tack slightly and see how to add components to an application using Visual Studio .NET. We'll see how to add components to the Toolbox, and then drag-and-drop component objects onto a new application. We'll also take a look at the source code that gets generated by the Component Designer, to create the component object in our application.

Adding a Component to the Toolbox in Visual Studio .NET

To add a component to the Toolbox in Visual Studio .NET, follow these steps:

❑ Launch Visual Studio .NET, and open the Toolbox if it is not already visible.

❑ Select one of the tabs on the Toolbox, to choose where to add the new component. The choice of available tabs depends on the type of project that is currently open in Visual Studio .NET. If in doubt, we suggest you select the General tab.

❑ Right-click on your chosen tab in the Toolbox, and select Customize Toolbox from the shortcut menu.

❑ The Customize Toolbox dialog box appears. Click the .NET Framework Components tab on the top of this dialog box, to display a list of .NET components. Click Browse, and navigate to the MyComponent.dll assembly file we created earlier. The dialog box displays information about the Employee component in this assembly, as follows:

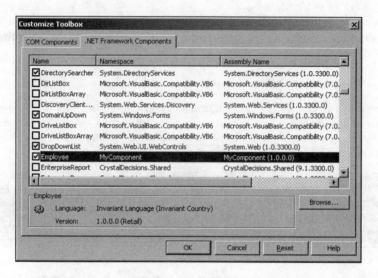

❏ Click OK, to add this Employee component to the Toolbox.

❏ Verify that the Employee component now appears in the Toolbox.

Adding Component Objects to an Application

Now that we've added the Employee component to the Toolbox in Visual Studio .NET, we can drag-and-drop Employee component objects onto our applications. Follow these steps:

❏ In Visual Studio .NET, create a new Visual Basic .NET Windows Application (for example).

❏ Select the Form component in Visual Designer. Change its (Name) property to something more meaningful, such as TestEmployeeForm. Also change its Text property to Test Employee Form. Finally, rename the source file Form1.vb to TestEmployeeForm.vb.

❏ Drag-and-drop an Employee component object onto the Visual Designer for the form. This causes the Component Designer to add code to our application, to create an Employee component object. The new component is displayed in the component tray in the Visual Designer. The properties for the Employee component object are shown in the Properties window:

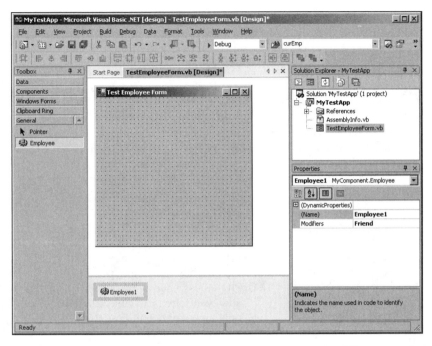

❑   View the source code file for TestEmployeeForm.vb. The following code has been generated to create an Employee component object and associate it with a Container object. Visual Studio .NET only creates the Container object if we add one or more components to the form.

As you may recall from our earlier discussion about the Employee class, the Employee constructor invokes the Add() method on the Container object, to add the component object to the container.

```
Friend WithEvents Employee1 As MyComponent.Employee

<System.Diagnostics.DebuggerStepThrough()> _
Private Sub InitializeComponent()

    Me.components = New System.ComponentModel.Container()
    Me.Employee1 = New MyComponent.Employee(Me.components)
    '
    ' TestEmployeeForm
    '
    Me.AutoScaleBaseSize = New System.Drawing.Size(5, 13)
    Me.ClientSize = New System.Drawing.Size(292, 273)
    Me.Name = "TestEmployeeForm"
    Me.Text = "Test Employee Form"

End Sub
```

199

Well, that was remarkably painless. Driven on by a sense of unbridled success, the next section shows how to define properties in a component class, and describes how to use attributes to make these properties accessible at design time to the Visual Designer.

Defining Properties and Events for a Component

When we add properties and events to a component, we should annotate these members with attributes to enable Visual Studio .NET to display the members correctly at design time. The following table describes the attributes we're going to use in our example. All of these attribute classes are defined in the `System.ComponentModel` namespace. See Visual Studio .NET Help for a complete list of attribute classes in this namespace.

Attributes used in this example	Description
`<Browsable()>`	Indicates that a property or event is browsable at design time; in other words, the property or event appears in the Properties window. By default, properties and events are browsable. Therefore, the only time you need to use this attribute is to prevent a member from being browsable: in this case, specify `<Browsable(False)>`.
`<Category()>`	Indicates that a property or event belongs to a particular category. Items in the same category are grouped together in the Properties window. If we don't specify a category, the property or event will be added to a category named `Misc` by default.
`<DefaultEvent()>`	This attribute is used on a class or structure definition, to indicate the default event in the class.
`<DefaultProperty()>`	This attribute is used on a class or structure definition, to indicate the default property in the class.
`<DefaultValue()>`	Indicates the default value for a property. If the property currently has this value, it is shown unbolded in the Properties window. If the property has a different value, it is displayed in bold. Note that if we don't specify a default value, the Properties window will always show the property in bold.

Attributes used in this example	Description
`<Description()>`	Provides a design time textual description of the property.
`<ParenthesizePropertyName()>`	Indicates that the property name should be displayed in parentheses. For example, the standard UI controls in .NET display the `Name` property in parentheses: `(Name)`.
`<ReadOnlyAttribute()>`	Indicates that the property is read-only at design time. If we omit this attribute, and the property has 'get' and 'set' property procedures, the property is deemed to be not read-only. Note that if the property doesn't have a 'set' property procedure, the property will be deemed to be read-only regardless of whether we specify this attribute.
`<RefreshProperties()>`	This attribute tells the Visual Designer how to refresh the display of other properties in the Properties window, if the user changes the value of this property. For example, `<RefreshProperties( RefreshProperties.All)>` indicates that all the properties are to be refreshed. This is useful if there are other properties that depend on the value of this property.
`<TypeConverter()>`	This attribute is used on a class or structure definition, to indicate the name of the type converter class to use for data conversions on this type.

Now that we've discussed which attributes we need, let's add some events and properties to the `Employee` component class. We'll begin by defining the default event and default property in the `Employee` class (we'll introduce the `SalaryChanged` event and the `FullName` property shortly):

```
<DefaultEvent("SalaryChanged"), _
  DefaultProperty("FullName")> _
Public Class Employee
    Inherits System.ComponentModel.Component

    ' Members...

End Class
```

Next, let's define some fields in the `Employee` class, to hold employee information. These fields use a combination of simple types (such as `String`) and more interesting types (such as `DateTime`, `Color`, and an array of `String`s). Also, we've initialized some of these fields for added excitement:

```
' Personal details
Private mFullName As String = "Name Unknown"
Private mDob As DateTime = DateTime.Today

' Employment details
Private mSalary As Double = 0.0
Private mSkills As String()
Private mCarColor As Color
```

We can define properties to expose the aforementioned fields at design time and at runtime. We'll introduce each property separately, to highlight the interesting attributes on each property:

❑ The `FullName` property has a `<DefaultValue("Name Unknown")>` attribute, to match the initial value of the `mFullName` field:

```
<Category("Personal details"), _
 Description("The employee's fullname"), _
 DefaultValue("Name Unknown")> _
Public Property FullName() As String
  Get
    Return mFullName
  End Get
  Set(ByVal Value As String)
    mFullName = Value
  End Set
End Property
```

❑ The `DateOfBirth` property, shown below, has a `<RefreshProperties(RefreshProperties.All)>` attribute. Whenever the user changes this property in the Properties window, all the other properties will be refreshed too. You'll see why this is important when we introduce an `Age` property in a moment.

```
<Category("Personal details"), _
 Description("The employee's date of birth"), _
 RefreshProperties(RefreshProperties.All)> _
Public Property DateOfBirth() As DateTime
  Get
    Return mDob
  End Get
  Set(ByVal Value As DateTime)
    mDob = Value
  End Set
End Property
```

The .NET class library defines an editor class named `DateTimeEditor` *in the* `System.ComponentModel.Design` *namespace, to allow* `DateTime` *values to be edited graphically in the Properties window. There is no need for us to use the* `<Editor()>` *attribute when we define* `DateTime` *properties, unless we want to specify a different editor class to edit this property). The* `DateTimeEditor` *has the following appearance:*

❑ The `Age` property displays the employee's current age. This is a read-only value, and is calculated by subtracting the employee's date of birth from the current date. Therefore, the `Age` property has to be refreshed if the `DateOfBirth` property changes. This explains why we annotated the `DateOfBirth` property with `<RefreshProperties(RefreshProperties.All)>`.

```
<Category("Personal details"), _
 Description("The employee's age (calculated from Date Of Birth)"), _
 ReadOnlyAttribute(True), _
 ParenthesizePropertyName(True)> _
Public ReadOnly Property Age() As Integer
  Get
    Dim years As Integer = Date.Today.Year - mDob.Year
    If Date.Today.DayOfYear < mDob.DayOfYear Then
      years -= 1
    End If
    Return years
  End Get
End Property
```

❑ The `Salary` property is entirely innocuous...

```
<Category("Employment details"), _
 Description("The employee's total annual salary"), _
 DefaultValue(0.0)> _
Public Property Salary() As Double
  Get
    Return mSalary
  End Get
  Set(ByVal Value As Double)
    mSalary = Value
  End Set
End Property
```

❑ The Skills property gets and sets an array of strings, representing the employee's skill set. There is no problem using array types with properties.

```
<Category("Employment details"), _
 Description("An array of strings, containing employee's skills")> _
Public Property Skills() As String()
  Get
    Return mSkills
  End Get
  Set(ByVal Value As String())
    mSkills = Value
  End Set
End Property
```

The .NET class library defines an editor class named ArrayEditor *in the* System.ComponentModel.Design *namespace, to allow arrays to be edited graphically in the Properties window. The* ArrayEditor *has the following appearance:*

❑ The CarColor property gets and sets a Color value.

```
<Category("Employment details"), _
 Description("The color of the employee's company car")> _
Public Property CarColor() As Color
  Get
    Return mCarColor
  End Get
  Set(ByVal Value As Color)
    mCarColor = Value
  End Set
End Property
```

The .NET class library defines an editor class named ColorEditor *in the* System.Drawing.Design *namespace, to allow* Color *values to be edited graphically via a palette in the Properties window. The* ColorEditor *has the following appearance (if we don't set the color, the editor displays the color as white by default):*

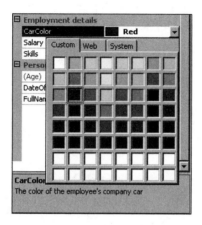

The next step is to define some events in the Employee class, to indicate when an employee's salary changes, and when the employee becomes a higher-rate tax payer (due to a healthy pay raise) or a lower-rate tax payer (due to cuts in operating costs in the company).

❑ The first step is to define an EmployeeEventArgs class, to provide information about the event. All the events raised in the Employee class will use EmployeeEventArgs as part of the event signature. EmployeeEventArgs class is shown below; this source code is available in EmployeeEventArgs.vb in the ch06\MyFinalComponent download folder:

```
Imports System

Public Class EmployeeEventArgs
  Inherits EventArgs

  ' Private fields
  Private mEmployeeName As String
  Private mEmployeeSalary As Double

  ' Constructor, to initialize private fields
  Public Sub New(ByVal EmployeeName As String, _
                 ByVal EmployeeSalary As Double)
    mEmployeeName = EmployeeName
    mEmployeeSalary = EmployeeSalary
  End Sub
```

```
' Properties, to get the values held in the private fields
Public ReadOnly Property EmployeeName() As String
  Get
    Return mEmployeeName
  End Get
End Property

Public ReadOnly Property EmployeeSalary() As Double
  Get
    Return mEmployeeSalary
  End Get
End Property

End Class
```

❑   We can now define a delegate in `Employee.vb`, to specify the signature
    for all events raised in the `Employee` class:

```
Public Delegate Sub EmployeeEventHandler( _
                    ByVal Source As Employee, _
                    ByVal e As EmployeeEventArgs)
```

❑   The `Employee` class will raise three events, as follows:

```
Public Event SalaryChanged       As EmployeeEventHandler
Public Event HigherRateTaxPayer As EmployeeEventHandler
Public Event LowerRateTaxPayer  As EmployeeEventHandler
```

❑   Let's write some methods to raise these events when the employee's salary
    changes. We've specified $100,000 as an arbitrary threshold for tax
    payment; if the employee earns this amount or more, he or she pays a
    higher rate of tax. Of course, this is an entirely unrealistic taxation model;
    taxes in the real world are much more complicated that this!

```
Private Shared mTaxThreshold As Double = 100000.0

Public Sub PayRaise(ByVal Amount As Double)

  Dim OriginalSalary As Double = mSalary
  mSalary += Amount

  RaiseEvent SalaryChanged(Me, _
                    New EmployeeEventArgs(mFullName, mSalary))

  If (mSalary >= mTaxThreshold) And _
      Not (OriginalSalary >= mTaxThreshold) Then
```

```
     RaiseEvent HigherRateTaxPayer(Me, _
                         New EmployeeEventArgs(mFullName, mSalary))
   End If

End Sub

Public Sub PayCut(ByVal Amount As Double)

   Dim OriginalSalary As Double = mSalary
   mSalary -= Amount

   RaiseEvent SalaryChanged(Me, _
                     New EmployeeEventArgs(mFullName, mSalary))

   If (mSalary < mTaxThreshold) And _
       Not (OriginalSalary < mTaxThreshold) Then

     RaiseEvent LowerRateTaxPayer(Me, _
                       New EmployeeEventArgs(mFullName, mSalary))
   End If

End Sub
```

Defining Converter Classes for Components

To complete the implementation of our Employee component, we'll add fields and properties to represent the employee's telephone numbers and home address. We'll write two new classes named TelephoneNumber and Address to encapsulate these details. We'll also write two converter classes named TelephoneNumberConverter and AddressConverter, to allow TelephoneNumber properties and Address properties to be displayable and editable in the Properties window.

Defining the TelephoneNumber Class

Let's begin with the TelephoneNumber class. For the sake of simplicity, our example assumes US-formatted numbers such as (123) 456-7890; in an industrial strength application, we'd probably need to cater for the wider world too! We might also want to perform some intelligent error checking, such as testing the area code to make sure it's valid.

This source code is available in TelephoneNumber.vb in the ch06\MyFinalComponent download folder. The <TypeConverter(GetType(TelephoneNumberConverter))> attribute at the start of the TelephoneNumber class definition associates the TelephoneNumberConverter converter class with TelephoneNumber:

207

```
Imports System
Imports System.ComponentModel

<TypeConverter(GetType(TelephoneNumberConverter))> _
Public Class TelephoneNumber

    Private mAreaCode As String
    Private mLocalNumber As String

    Public Sub New(ByVal AreaCode As String, _
                   ByVal LocalNumber As String)
      mAreaCode = AreaCode
      mLocalNumber = LocalNumber
    End Sub

    Public Property AreaCode() As String
      Get
        Return mAreaCode
      End Get
      Set(ByVal Value As String)
        mAreaCode = Value
      End Set
    End Property

    Public Property LocalNumber() As String
      Get
        Return mLocalNumber
      End Get
      Set(ByVal Value As String)
        mLocalNumber = Value
      End Set
    End Property

End Class
```

Defining the TelephoneNumberConverter Class

The `TelephoneNumberConverter` class illustrates the general rules for defining
converter classes. You can download this source code from
`TelephoneNumberConverter.vb`. Converter classes are quite technical little beasties,
so we'll take this a step at a time:

❑   As ever, we begin with a clutch of `Imports` statements:

```
Imports System                      ' For misc .NET types
Imports System.ComponentModel       ' For misc ComponentModel types
Imports System.Globalization        ' For ICultureInfo
Imports System.ComponentModel.Design.Serialization
                                    ' For InstanceDescriptor
Imports System.Text.RegularExpressions ' For Regex, to parse telnums
Imports System.Reflection           ' For ConstructorInfo
```

❑ Here is the definition of the `TelephoneNumberConverter` class. All converter classes inherit from `System.ComponentModel.TypeConverter`:

```
Public Class TelephoneNumberConverter
  Inherits TypeConverter

  ' Members ...

End Class
```

❑ The first method we're going to implement is `CanConvertFrom()`. This method indicates whether `TelephoneNumber` object can be created from some other data type. For example, the Visual Designer calls this method to establish whether `TelephoneNumber` objects can be created from a string value.

It's up to us to choose what data types we're prepared to convert from. The way we've implemented the method indicates we're definitely prepared to convert from a string. For any other data type, we pass the question back up to our base class.

```
Public Overloads Overrides Function CanConvertFrom( _
                ByVal context As ITypeDescriptorContext, _
                ByVal sourceType As Type) As Boolean

  If sourceType Is GetType(String) Then
    Return True
  Else
    Return MyBase.CanConvertFrom(context, sourceType)
  End If

End Function
```

❑ The next method on our to-do list is `ConvertFrom()`. This method receives a parameter of some compatible data type (as established by a prior call to `CanConvertFrom()`). The method must use the supplied value to create and return a `TelephoneNumber` with a corresponding value.

The way we've implemented this method, we expect a string in the format `(123) 456-7890`; the parentheses, space character, and dash are optional. We use a Regular Expression to extract the area code and local number from this string, and then create and return a `TelephoneNumber` object with these values.

For more information about Regular Expressions, see Wrox' Visual Basic .NET Text Manipulation Handbook: String Handling and Regular Expressions (ISBN 1861007-30-2).

```
Public Overloads Overrides Function ConvertFrom( _
                  ByVal context As ITypeDescriptorContext, _
                  ByVal culture As CultureInfo, _
                  ByVal value As Object) As Object

  If TypeOf value Is String Then

    Dim m As Match = Regex.Match( _
      CStr(value), _
      "\(?(?<area>\d{1,3})\)?\s?(?<local1>\d{3})-?(?<local2>\d{4})")

    Return New TelephoneNumber(m.Groups("area").Value, _
                               m.Groups("local1").Value & "-" & _
                               m.Groups("local2").Value)

  Else

      ' If the value-to-be-converted is not a String, pass the
      ' conversion request up to our base class
      Return MyBase.ConvertFrom(context, culture, value)

  End If

End Function
```

❑   The previous two methods dealt with the task of converting from some
    other data type into a TelphoneNumber. We must also write two methods
    to deal with conversions in the opposite direction, where we need to
    convert a TelephoneNumber object to some other type.

    Let's see the CanConvertTo() method first. This method indicates that
    TelephoneNumber objects can be converted into a string value or an
    InstanceDescriptor object. We'll describe InstanceDescriptor in
    a moment.

```
Public Overloads Overrides Function CanConvertTo( _
                  ByVal context As ITypeDescriptorContext, _
                  ByVal destinationType As Type) As Boolean

  If (destinationType Is GetType(String)) Or _
     (destinationType Is GetType(InstanceDescriptor)) Then

    Return True

  Else

      ' If the destinationType is not String or InstanceDescriptor,
      ' pass the conversion request up to our base class
      Return MyBase.CanConvertFrom(context, destinationType)

  End If

End Function
```

❑ The ConvertTo() method performs these conversions from a TelephoneNumber object into a string value or an InstanceDescriptor object. The string conversion is quite simple; the conversion yields a string in the format "(123) 456-7890".

The InstanceDescriptor conversion is much more complicated. An InstanceDescriptor object is like a playback object; it contains information about how to create TelephoneNumber objects in source code. We must tell the InstanceDescriptor which constructor to call, and what parameter values to use in that constructor.

The Visual Designer uses the information in the InstanceDescriptor object to generate source code in the InitializeComponents method in the host application. This source code creates a TelephoneNumber object and initializes it with the values we specified in the Properties window.

```
Public Overloads Overrides Function ConvertTo( _
                ByVal context As ITypeDescriptorContext, _
                ByVal culture As CultureInfo, _
                ByVal value As Object, _
                ByVal destinationType As Type) As Object

   If destinationType Is GetType(String) Then

      Dim tn As TelephoneNumber = CType(value, TelephoneNumber)
      If tn Is Nothing Then
        Return ""
      Else
        Return String.Format("({0}) {1}", tn.AreaCode, tn.LocalNumber)
      End If

   ElseIf destinationType Is GetType(InstanceDescriptor) Then

      Dim ci As ConstructorInfo
      ci = GetType(TelephoneNumber).GetConstructor( _
                New Type() {GetType(String), GetType(String)})

      Dim tn As TelephoneNumber = CType(value, TelephoneNumber)

      Return New InstanceDescriptor( _
                ci, New Object() {tn.AreaCode, tn.LocalNumber})
   Else

      Return MyBase.ConvertTo(context, culture, value, destinationType)

   End If

End Function
```

That concludes the implementation of the `TelephoneNumberConverter` and `TelephoneNumber` classes. We are now ready to add some `TelephoneNumber` fields and properties to the `Employee` class. We'll add three `TelephoneNumber` fields, to hold the employee's work number, cell phone number, and home number. In a real application, we might also allow the employee to have additional numbers such as a fax number, a pager number, and so on:

```
<DefaultEvent("SalaryChanged"), _
 DefaultProperty("FullName")> _
Public Class Employee
  Inherits System.ComponentModel.Component

  ' Telephone numbers
  Private mHomeNumber As TelephoneNumber
  Private mWorkNumber As TelephoneNumber
  Private mCellNumber As TelephoneNumber

  <Category("Telephone numbers"), _
   Description("The employee's work telephone number")> _
  Public Property WorkNumber() As TelephoneNumber
    Get
      Return mWorkNumber
    End Get
    Set(ByVal Value As TelephoneNumber)
      mWorkNumber = Value
    End Set
  End Property

  <Category("Telephone numbers"), _
   Description("The employee's cell (mobile) telephone number")> _
  Public Property CellNumber() As TelephoneNumber
    Get
      Return mCellNumber
    End Get
    Set(ByVal Value As TelephoneNumber)
      mCellNumber = Value
    End Set
  End Property

  <Category("Telephone numbers"), _
   Description("The employee's home telephone number")> _
  Public Property HomeNumber() As TelephoneNumber
    Get
      Return mHomeNumber
    End Get
    Set(ByVal Value As TelephoneNumber)
      mHomeNumber = Value
    End Set
  End Property

  ' Plus other members, as before

End Class
```

The following screenshot shows how these `TelephoneNumber` properties will appear in the Properties window:

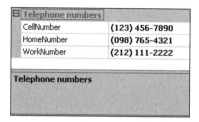

Defining the Address Class

We can now turn our attention to the `Address` class. This source code is available in `Address.vb` in the `ch06\MyFinalComponent` download folder.

Let's view the `Address` class first, and then pick out a couple of important features. For the sake of simplicity, our `Address` class just holds the employee's street name, city, and country; in an industrial strength application, we'd probably need to store additional information such as the state (or area) and zipcode (or postal code):

```
Imports System
Imports System.ComponentModel

<TypeConverter(GetType(AddressConverter))> _
Public Class Address

    Private mStreet As String
    Private mCity As String
    Private mCountry As String

    Public Sub New(ByVal Street As String, _
                   ByVal City As String, _
                   ByVal Country As String)
      mStreet = Street
      mCity = City
      mCountry = Country
    End Sub

    <RefreshProperties(RefreshProperties.All)> _
    Public Property Street() As String
      Get
         Return mStreet
      End Get
      Set(ByVal Value As String)
         mStreet = Value
      End Set
    End Property
```

```
    <RefreshProperties(RefreshProperties.All)> _
    Public Property City() As String
      Get
        Return mCity
      End Get
      Set(ByVal Value As String)
        mCity = Value
      End Set
    End Property

    <RefreshProperties(RefreshProperties.All)> _
    Public Property Country() As String
      Get
        Return mCountry
      End Get
      Set(ByVal Value As String)
        mCountry = Value
      End Set
    End Property

  End Class
```

Notice the `<TypeConverter(GetType(AddressConverter))>` attribute at the start of the `Address` class definition, to associate the `AddressConverter` converter class with `Address`. We'll see the `AddressConverter` class shortly.

Also notice that each of the properties in the `Address` class is prefixed with a `<RefreshProperties(RefreshProperties.All)>` attribute. The reason we've done this is because we want the `Street`, `City`, or `Country` properties to be editable individually in the Properties window, as follows:

HomeAddress	1 Main Street, Midville, USA
Street	1 Main Street
City	Midville
Country	USA

The `<RefreshProperties(RefreshProperties.All)>` attribute ensures that if the user changes the `Street`, `City`, or `Country` properties in an address, all the other properties in the Properties window will be refreshed too, including the `HomeAddress` property in the `Employee` component (we'll add the `HomeAddress` property to the `Employee` class shortly).

Defining the AddressConverter Class

The `AddressConverter` class is available in `AddressConverter.vb` in the `ch06\MyFinalComponent` download folder. The class is similar in scope and intent to the `TelephoneNumberConverter` class we saw earlier. Here's the outline for the class:

```
Imports System                          ' For misc .NET types
Imports System.ComponentModel           ' For misc ComponentModel types
Imports System.Globalization            ' For ICultureInfo
Imports System.ComponentModel.Design.Serialization
                                        ' For InstanceDescriptor
Imports System.Reflection               ' For ConstructorInfo


Public Class AddressConverter
    Inherits TypeConverter

    ' Conversion class methods and properties (discussed below...)

End Class
```

The class requires a `CanConvertFrom()` method, to allow conversions from string values into `Address` objects. The class also requires a `ConvertFrom()` method, to perform conversions from string values into `Address` objects. The string is expected to be formatted as `streetname, cityname, countryname`.

```
Public Overloads Overrides Function CanConvertFrom( _
                ByVal context As ITypeDescriptorContext, _
                ByVal sourceType As Type) As Boolean

   If sourceType Is GetType(String) Then
      Return True
   Else
      Return MyBase.CanConvertFrom(context, sourceType)
   End If
End Function


Public Overloads Overrides Function ConvertFrom( _
                ByVal context As ITypeDescriptorContext, _
                ByVal culture As CultureInfo, _
                ByVal value As Object) As Object

   If TypeOf value Is String Then
      Dim str As String = CStr(value)
      Dim strings As String() = str.Split(New Char() {","c})
      Return New Address(strings(0), strings(1), strings(2))
   Else
      Return MyBase.ConvertFrom(context, culture, value)
   End If

End Function
```

The `CanConvertTo()` method, shown below, allows `Address` objects to be converted into string values and `InstanceDescriptor` objects. The `ConvertTo()` method performs conversions from an `Address` object into a string or an `InstanceDescriptor` object, as appropriate. Notice that the `ConvertTo()` method performs some rudimentary error checking and formatting for string values.

```
Public Overloads Overrides Function CanConvertTo( _
                  ByVal context As ITypeDescriptorContext, _
                  ByVal destinationType As Type) As Boolean

  If (destinationType Is GetType(String)) Or _
     (destinationType Is GetType(InstanceDescriptor)) Then
    Return True
  Else
    Return MyBase.CanConvertFrom(context, destinationType)
  End If

End Function
```

```
Public Overloads Overrides Function ConvertTo( _
                  ByVal context As ITypeDescriptorContext, _
                  ByVal culture As CultureInfo, _
                  ByVal value As Object, _
                  ByVal destinationType As Type) As Object

  If destinationType Is GetType(String) Then

    Dim addr As Address = CType(value, Address)
    Dim street, city, country As String
    If (addr.Street Is Nothing) Or (addr.Street = "") Then
      street = "<street>"
    Else
      street = addr.Street
    End If
    If (addr.City Is Nothing) Or (addr.City = "") Then
      city = "<city>"
    Else
      city = addr.City
    End If
    If (addr.Country Is Nothing) Or (addr.Country = "") Then
      country = "<country>"
    Else
      country = addr.Country
    End If

    Return street & ", " & city & ", " & country

  ElseIf destinationType Is GetType(InstanceDescriptor) Then

    Dim ci As ConstructorInfo
    ci = GetType(Address).GetConstructor( _
      New Type(){GetType(String), GetType(String), GetType(String)})

    Dim addr As Address = CType(value, Address)
    Return New InstanceDescriptor( _
      ci, New Object() {addr.Street, addr.City, addr.Country})
```

```
Else

    Return MyBase.ConvertTo(context, culture, value, destinationType)

End If

End Function
```

Finally, the `AddressConverter` class requires two additional methods we haven't seen before:

- ❑ `GetPropertiesSupported()` indicates that `Address` objects have internal properties of their own, and that these properties should be displayed separately when an `Address` property is displayed in the Properties window.

```
Public Overloads Overrides Function GetPropertiesSupported( _
            ByVal context As ITypeDescriptorContext) As Boolean
    Return True
End Function
```

- ❑ `GetProperties()` returns a `PropertyDescriptionCollection`, containing information about all the internal properties inside `Address`. The Visual Designer queries the underlying class for these properties. Notice we've used the `Sort()` method to ensure these internal properties are displayed in the order `Street`, `City`, and `Country`.

```
Public Overloads Overrides Function GetProperties( _
            ByVal context As ITypeDescriptorContext, _
            ByVal value As Object, _
            ByVal attributes() As Attribute) _
                As PropertyDescriptorCollection

    Dim properties As PropertyDescriptorCollection
    properties = TypeDescriptor.GetProperties(GetType(Address))
    properties = properties.Sort( _
            New String() {"Street", "City", "Country"})
    Return properties

End Function

End Class
```

That concludes the implementation of the `AddressConverter` and `Address` classes. We are now ready to add some `Address` fields and properties to the `Employee` class:

```
<DefaultEvent("SalaryChanged"), _
 DefaultProperty("FullName")> _
Public Class Employee
   Inherits System.ComponentModel.Component

   Private mHomeAddress As New Address( _
                                 "<street>", "<city>", "<country>")

   <Category("Personal details"), _
    Description("The employee's home address")> _
   Public Property HomeAddress() As Address
      Get
         Return mHomeAddress
      End Get
      Set(ByVal Value As Address)
         mHomeAddress = Value
      End Set
   End Property

   ' Plus other members, as before

End Class
```

Testing the Final Employee Component Class

A final implementation of the Employee component class is available in the
ch06\MyFinalComponent download folder. We've also provided a sample test
application in the ch06\UseFinalComponent download folder.

The test application appears as follows in Visual Studio .NET. The application has a
single Employee component object, whose properties are displayed in the Properties
window. These properties exhibit the appearance and capabilities we've worked hard
to define during the chapter:

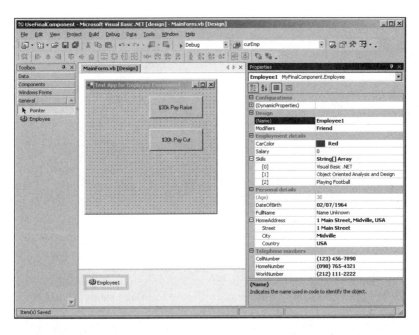

Here is a partial listing of some of the code generated by the Visual Designer, to achieve the property settings we specify in the Properties window. This code resides in MainForm.vb:

```vb
Public Class MainForm
    Inherits System.Windows.Forms.Form

    Friend WithEvents Employee1 As MyFinalComponent.Employee

    <System.Diagnostics.DebuggerStepThrough()> _
    Private Sub InitializeComponent()

        Me.Employee1 = _
            New MyFinalComponent.Employee(Me.components)

        Me.Employee1.CarColor = System.Drawing.Color.Red

        Me.Employee1.CellNumber = _
            New MyFinalComponent.TelephoneNumber("123", "456-7890")

        Me.Employee1.DateOfBirth = _
            New Date(1964, 7, 2, 0, 0, 0, 0)

        Me.Employee1.HomeAddress = _
            New MyFinalComponent.Address("1 Main Street", _
                                         "Midville", _
                                         "USA")
```

```
     Me.Employee1.HomeNumber = _
       New MyFinalComponent.TelephoneNumber("098", "765-4321")

     Me.Employee1.Skills = _
       New String() {"Visual Basic .NET", _
                      "Object Oriented Analysis and Design", _
                      "Playing Football"}

     Me.Employee1.WorkNumber = _
       New MyFinalComponent.TelephoneNumber("212", "111-2222")

     ' Plus other code

   End Sub

   ' Plus other members

End Class
```

The test application also exercises the events on the `Employee` component object.
Every time the user clicks one of the buttons on the form, the salary is changed and a
`SalaryChanged` event is raised. If the employee's salary goes above $100,000, a
`HigherRateTaxPayer` event is raised. If the employee's salary slips back below
$100,000, a `LowerRateTaxPayer` event is raised. Here are the event handler methods
for these events, along with the message boxes displayed for each event:

Here is the event handler method for the `SalaryChanged` event, along with the
message box that gets displayed when this event is handled:

```
Private Sub Employee1_SalaryChanged( _
               ByVal Source As MyFinalComponent.Employee, _
               ByVal e As MyFinalComponent.EmployeeEventArgs) _
                     Handles Employee1.SalaryChanged

  MessageBox.Show("New salary " & e.EmployeeSalary, _
               "Salary changed for " & e.EmployeeName)

End Sub
```

Here is the event handler method for the `HigherRateTaxPayer` event, together with
the associated message box for this event:

```
Private Sub Employee1_HigherRateTaxPayer( _
                    ByVal Source As MyFinalComponent.Employee, _
                    ByVal e As MyFinalComponent.EmployeeEventArgs) _
                            Handles Employee1.HigherRateTaxPayer

    MessageBox.Show("New salary " & e.EmployeeSalary, _
        e.EmployeeName & " has just become a higher-rate tax payer")

End Sub
```

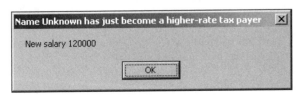

```
Private Sub Employee1_LowerRateTaxPayer( _
                    ByVal Source As MyFinalComponent.Employee, _
                    ByVal e As MyFinalComponent.EmployeeEventArgs) _
                            Handles Employee1.LowerRateTaxPayer

    MessageBox.Show("New salary " & e.EmployeeSalary, _
        e.EmployeeName & " has just become a lower-rate tax payer")

End Sub
```

Finally, here is the event handler method for the `LowerRateTaxPayer` event, together with the associated message box:

Summary

And so we come to the end of the final chapter in the book. We've covered a lot of ground, and provided much guidance on how and why to use reflection in .NET applications.

In this chapter, we've seen how to use the classes, interfaces, and attributes defined in the `System.ComponentModel` namespace. This namespace defines the following key interfaces, which allow us to create and use components in a consistent manner:

❑ The IComponent interface specifies the methods and properties required in component classes. A component class is any class that implements IComponent.

❑ The IContainer interface specifies the methods and properties required in container classes. A container class is any class that implements IContainer.

❑ The ISite interface specifies the glue between components and containers. Site objects facilitate communication between component objects and container objects.

The System.ComponentModel namespace also defines a veritable gamut of attribute classes, type converter classes, and descriptor classes. Here's a brief reminder of the roles of these classes:

❑ Attribute classes enable us to specify metadata on components, properties, events, and other member types. There are numerous attributes that allow us to provide designtime information for consumption by the Visual Designer.

❑ Type converter classes provide a standard infrastructure for querying the conversion capabilities to and from different types, and for performing these conversions. Type converter classes are used extensively by the Visual Designer, in order to display property and event information in the Properties window, and to generate source code to persist these settings.

❑ Descriptor classes open the gateway to a tremendously powerful and versatile style of generic programming. We can use descriptor classes to obtain full information about any type, and any of the members defined in these types.

VB.NET

Reflection

Handbook

Appendix

Support, Errata, and Code Download

We always value hearing from our readers, and we want to know what you think about this book and series: what you liked, what you didn't like, and what you think we can do better next time. You can send us your comments, either by returning the reply card in the back of the book, or by e-mailing us at feedback@wrox.com. Please be sure to mention the book title in your message.

How to Download the Sample Code for the Book

When you log on to the Wrox site, http://www.wrox.com/, simply locate the title through our Search facility or by using one of the title lists. Click on Download Code on the book's detail page.

The files that are available for download from our site have been archived using WinZip. When you have saved the attachments to a folder on your hard-drive, you will need to extract the files using WinZip, or a compatible tool. Inside the Zip file will be a folder structure and an HTML file that explains the structure and gives you further information, including links to e-mail support, and suggested further reading.

Errata

We've made every effort to ensure that there are no errors in the text or in the code. However, no one is perfect and mistakes can occur. If you find an error in this book, like a spelling mistake or a faulty piece of code, we would be very grateful for feedback. By sending in errata, you may save another reader hours of frustration, and of course, you will be helping us to provide even higher quality information. Simply e-mail the information to support@wrox.com, your information will be checked and if correct, posted to the Errata page for that title.

To find errata, locate this book on the Wrox web site (http://www.wrox.com/ACON11.asp?ISBN=1861007590), and click on the Book Errata link on the book's detail page.

E-Mail Support

If you wish to query a problem in the book with an expert who knows the book in detail then e-mail support@wrox.com, with the title of the book, and the last four numbers of the ISBN in the subject field of the e-mail. A typical e-mail should include the following:

❑   The name, last four digits of the ISBN, and page number of the problem, in the Subject field

❑   Your name, contact information, and the problem, in the body of the message

We won't send you junk mail. We need the details to save your time and ours. When you send an e-mail message, it will go through the following chain of support:

❑   **Customer Support**

Your message is delivered to our customer support staff. They have files on most frequently asked questions and will answer anything general about the book or the web site immediately.

❑   **Editorial**

More in-depth queries are forwarded to the technical editor responsible for that book. They have experience with the programming language or particular product, and are able to answer detailed technical questions on the subject. Once an issue has been resolved, the editor can post the errata to the web site.

❑   **The Author**

Finally, in the unlikely event that the editor cannot answer your problem, they will forward the request to the author. We do try to protect the author from any distractions to their writing (or programming); but we are quite happy to forward specific requests to them. All Wrox authors help with the support on their books. They will e-mail the customer and the editor with their response, and again all readers should benefit.

The Wrox support process can only offer support for issues that are directly pertinent to the content of our published title. Support for questions that fall outside the scope of normal book support, is provided via our P2P community lists – http://p2p.wrox.com/forum.

p2p.wrox.com

For author and peer discussion, join the P2P mailing lists. Our unique system provides Programmer to Programmer™ contact on mailing lists, forums, and newsgroups, all in addition to our one-to-one e-mail support system. Be confident that the many Wrox authors and other industry experts who are present on our mailing lists are examining any queries posted. At http://p2p.wrox.com/, you will find a number of different lists that will help you, not only while you read this book, but also as you develop your own applications.

To subscribe to a mailing list follow these steps:

- ❏ Go to http://p2p.wrox.com/
- ❏ Choose the appropriate category from the left menu bar
- ❏ Click on the mailing list you wish to join
- ❏ Follow the instructions to subscribe and fill in your e-mail address and password
- ❏ Reply to the confirmation e-mail you receive
- ❏ Use the subscription manager to join more lists and set your mail preferences

VB.NET

Reflection

Handbook

Index

Index

A Guide to the Index

The index is arranged hierarchically, in alphabetical order, with symbols preceding the letter A. Most second-level entries and many third-level entries also occur as first-level entries. This is to ensure that users will find the information they require however they choose to search for it.

binding (continued)
reflective late binding, 8
run-time binding, 11
syntactic late binding, 8
BindingFlags enumeration,
System.Reflection namespace
flag values, 38
GetField flag, 76
GetField method, Type class, 42
GetFields method, Type class, 42
GetProperties method, Type class, 44
GetProperty flag, 70
Instance value, 38, 96
InvokeMethod flag, 38, 64, 65
Public value, 96
SetField flag, 38, 76, 81
SetProperty flag, 38, 70, 75
book outline and readership, 1-2
BrowsableAttribute class,
System.ComponentModel namespace, 200
Build property, Version class, 94

C

CanConvertFrom method, TypeConverter
class, 215
CanConvertTo method, TypeConverter class,
210, 215
CanRead property, PropertyInfo class, 43
CanWrite property, PropertyInfo class, 43
CategoryAttribute class,
System.ComponentModel namespace,
182, 200
CharSet property, DllImportAttribute class, 140
class member metadata
examining, 36
Info objects, 36
Class value, AttributeTargets enumeration, 137
Class value, TypeAttributes enumeration, 130
client application
EDI invoicing and billing system, 114
code, downloading samples, 225
CodeBase property, Assembly class, 27
collection protocol, 8
ColorEditor class,
System.ComponentModel.Design
namespace, 205
ComboBox class, System.Windows.Forms
namespace
SelectedIndexChanged method, 79
SelectedItem property, 80
compilation
controlling using attributes, 143
compile-time type, 13
Component class, System.ComponentModel
namespace
Control class inherits from, 167

Dispose method, 187
implementing IComponent interface, 183
Component Designer
building components, 185
generating constructors, 186
InitializeComponent method, 187
ComponentCollection class,
System.ComponentModel namespace, 190
components
building
access modifiers, 183
defining as nested class, 184
Visual Studio .NET, 184
with System.ComponentModel, 181
Employee example, 181
controls as type of component, 167
defining, 182
custom class to host components, 191
MyComplexContainer example, 192
converter classes, 207
definition, 166
hosting in Container class, 189
MySimpleContainer example, 189
storing in a container, 181, 188
Toolbox
adding to, 182
using from, 187
Visual Studio .NET, 197
Components property, Container class, 190
Concrete classes, 99
compared to Abstract classes, 99
EDI invoicing and billing system, 111
VendorTransform concrete classes, 111
VendorUploadNotify concrete classes, 111
implementing Abstract Factory Pattern, 99
ConditionalAttribute class,
System.Diagnostics namespace, 120, 143
controlling compilation using attributes, 143
viewing MSIL using Disassembler, 145, 147
Debug preprocessor identifier and, 143
defining Debug preprocessor symbol, 146
without defining Debug preprocessor
symbol, 145
configuration file
EDI invoicing and billing system, 104
Constructor value, AttributeTargets
enumeration, 137
ConstructorInfo class, System.Reflection
namespace, 19, 36, 48
retrieving constructors of Employee class, 48
Container class, System.ComponentModel
namespace, 181
Add method, 190
Components property, 190
hosting components, 189
MySimpleContainer example, 189
implements IContainer interface, 188
Remove method, 190
containers
definition, 167
storing components, 188

Visual Basic .NET Threading Handbook

Authors: Ardestani, Ferracchiati, Gopikrishna, Redkar, Sivakumar, Titus
ISBN: 1-861007-13-2
US$ 29.99
Can$ 46.99

All .NET languages now have access to the Free Threading Model that many
Visual Basic Developers have been waiting for. Compared to the earlier apartment
threading model, this gives you much finer control over where to implement
threading and what you are given access to. It also provides several new ways for
your application to spin out of control.

This handbook explains how to avoid some common pitfalls when designing multi-
threaded applications by presenting some guidelines for good design practice. By
investigating the .NET threading model architecture, you will be able to make sure
that your applications take full advantage of it.

What you will learn from this book
- Thread creation
- Using timers to schedule threads to execute at specified intervals
- Synchronizing thread execution - avoiding deadlocks and race
  conditions
- Spinning threads from within threads, and synchronizing them
- Modeling your applications to a specific thread design model
- Scaling threaded applications by using the ThreadPool class
- Tracing your threaded application's execution in order to debug it

Visual Basic .NET Text Manipulation Handbook:
String Handling and Regular Expressions

Authors: François Liger, Craig McQueen, Paul Wilton
ISBN: 1-861007-30-2
US$ 29.99
Can$ 46.99

Text forms an integral part of many applications. Earlier versions of Visual Basic would hide from you the intricacies of how text was being handled, limiting your ability to control your program's execution or performance. The .NET Framework gives you much finer control.

This handbook takes an in-depth look at the text manipulation classes that are included within the .NET Framework, in all cases providing you with invaluable information as to their relative performance merits. The String and Stringbuilder classes are investigated and the newly acquired support for regular expressions is illustrated in detail.

What you will learn from this book
- String representation and management within the .NET Framework
- Using the StringBuilder object to improve application performance
- Choosing between the different object methods when manipulating text
- How to safely convert between String and other data types
- How to take advantage of .NET's Unicode representation of text for Internationalization
- The use of regular expressions including syntax and pattern matching to optimize your text manipulation operations

Visual Basic .NET Class Design Handbook:
Coding Effective Classes

Authors: Andy Olsen, Damon Allison, James Speer
ISBN: 1-861007-08-6
US$ 29.99
Can$ 46.99

Designing effective classes that you do not need to revisit and revise over and over again is an art. Within the .NET Framework, whatever code you write in Visual Basic .NET is encapsulated within the class hierarchy of the .NET Framework.

By investigating in depth the various members a class can contain, this handbook aims to give you a deep understanding of the implications of all the decisions you can make at design time. This book will equip you with the necessary knowledge to build classes that are robust, flexible, and reusable.

What you will learn from this book
- The role of types in .NET
- The different kinds of type we can create in VB.NET
- How VB.NET defines type members
- The fundamental role of methods as containers of program logic
- The role of constructors and their effective use
- Object cleanup and disposal
- When and how to use properties and indexers to encapsulate data
- How .NET's event system works
- How to control and exploit inheritance in our types
- The logical and physical code organisation through namespaces and assemblies